Hidden Freedom

Colorblind Black & White Photography

Joseph Fleming

Being colorblind gives an advantage when composing black & white… less confusion.

This special collection exhibits the lonely freedom of a hidden perspective selected from thousands of captures during years of travels. All images were framed in the camera and presented without edits, genuine as seen through the lens. Panchromatic conversion applied by proprietary process.

Original fine art and custom work available.

info@ BEACHNOISE.com

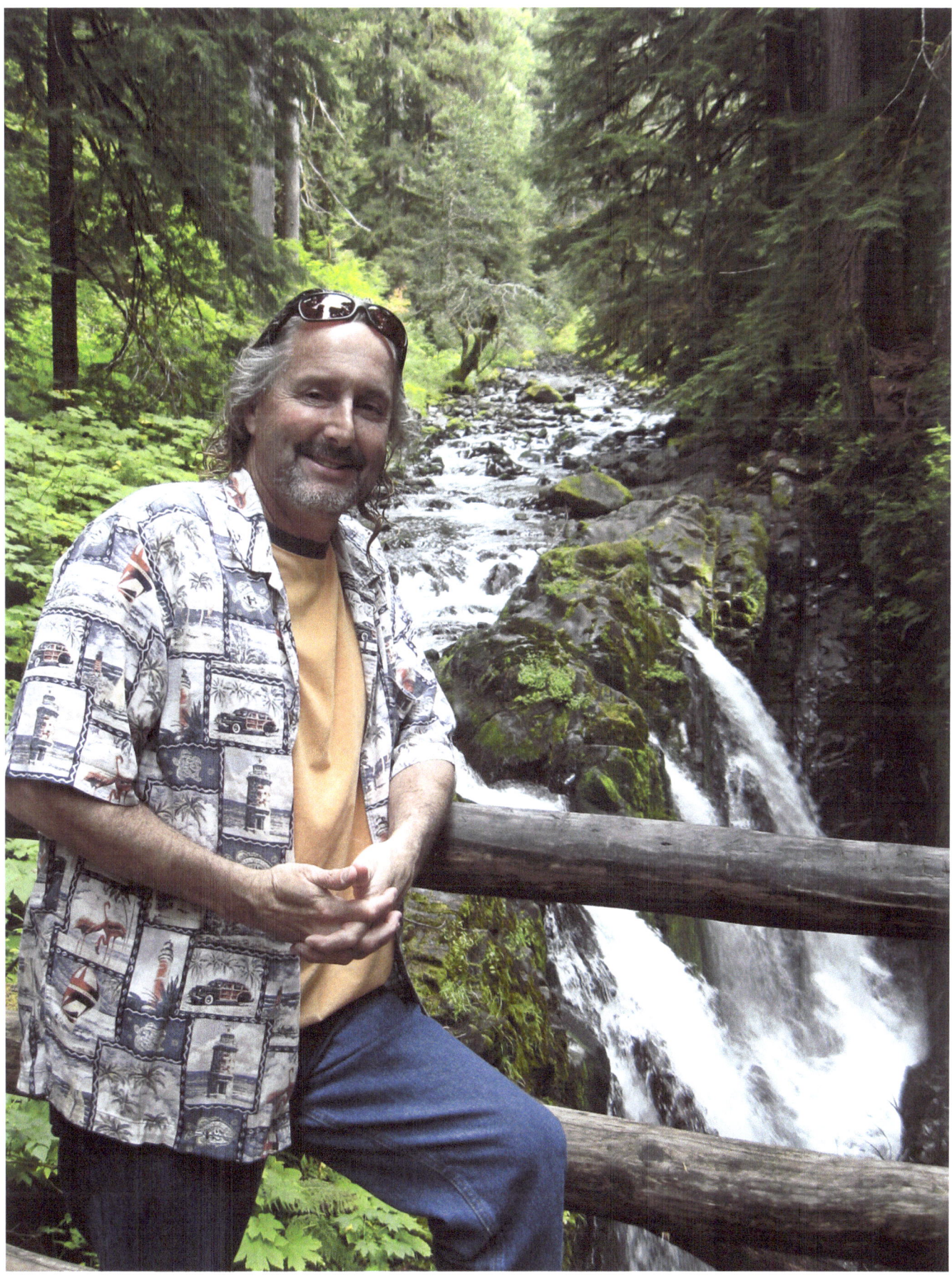

0125

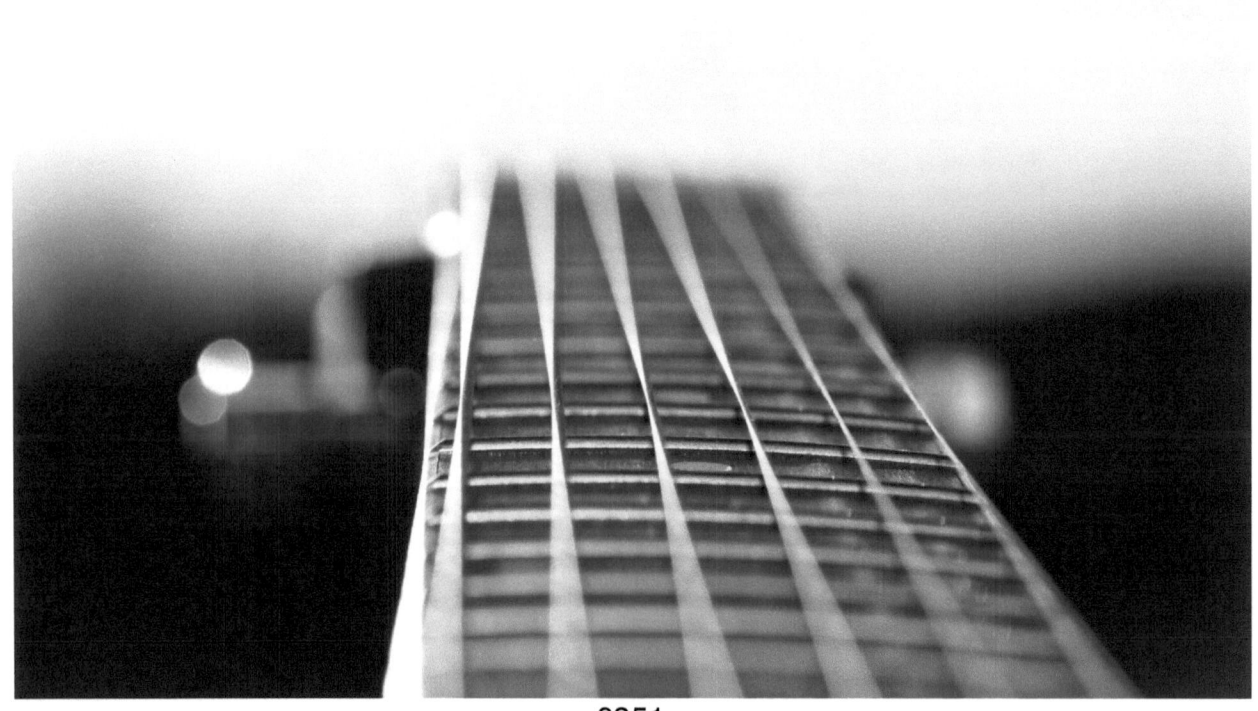

0351

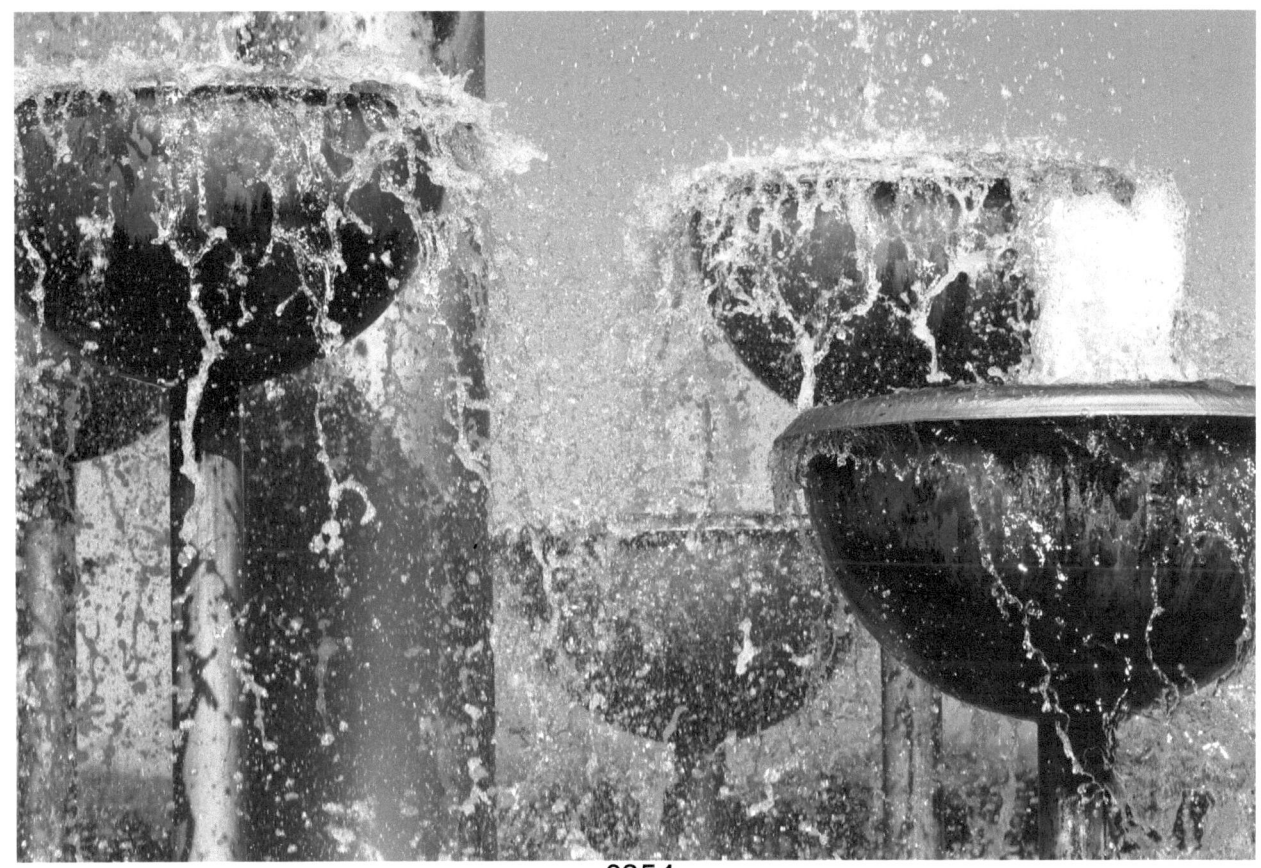

0354

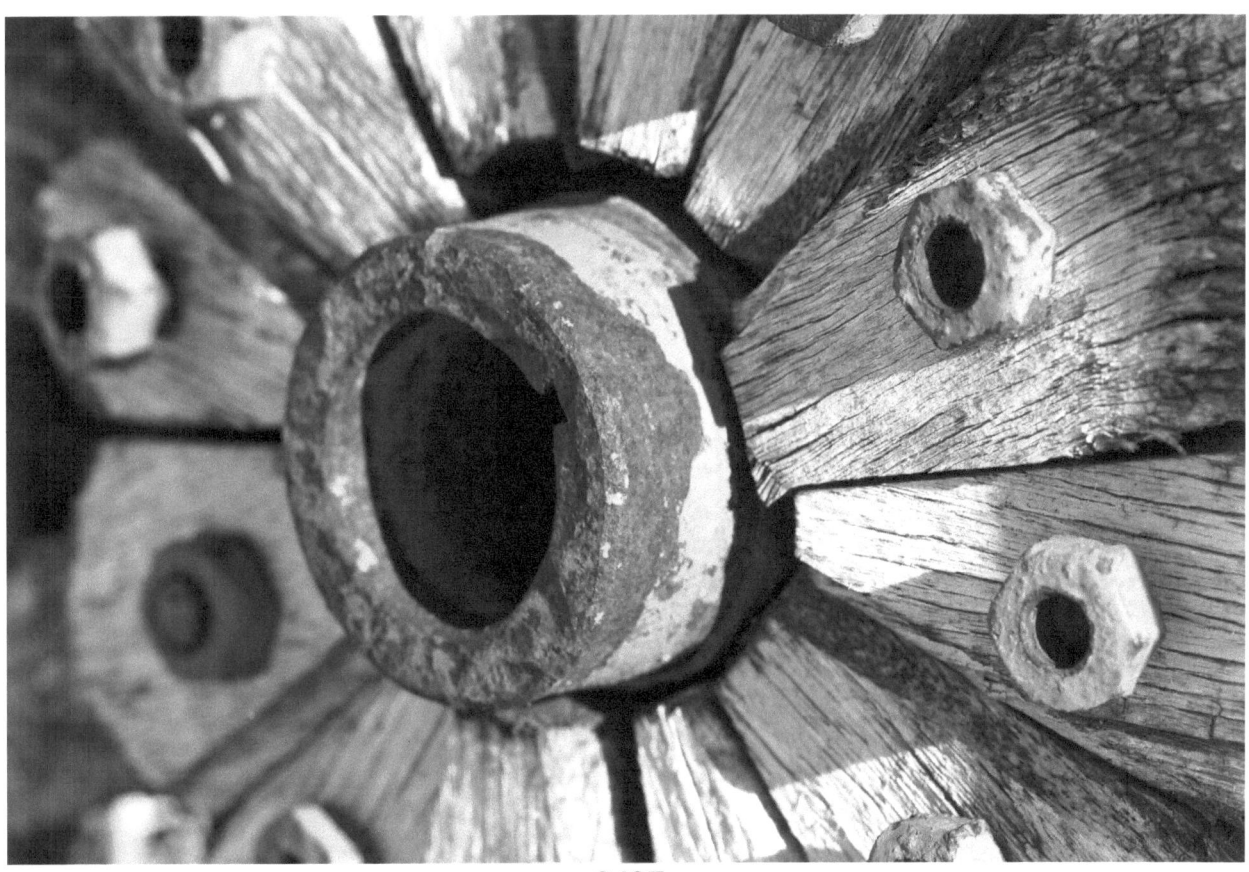

0437

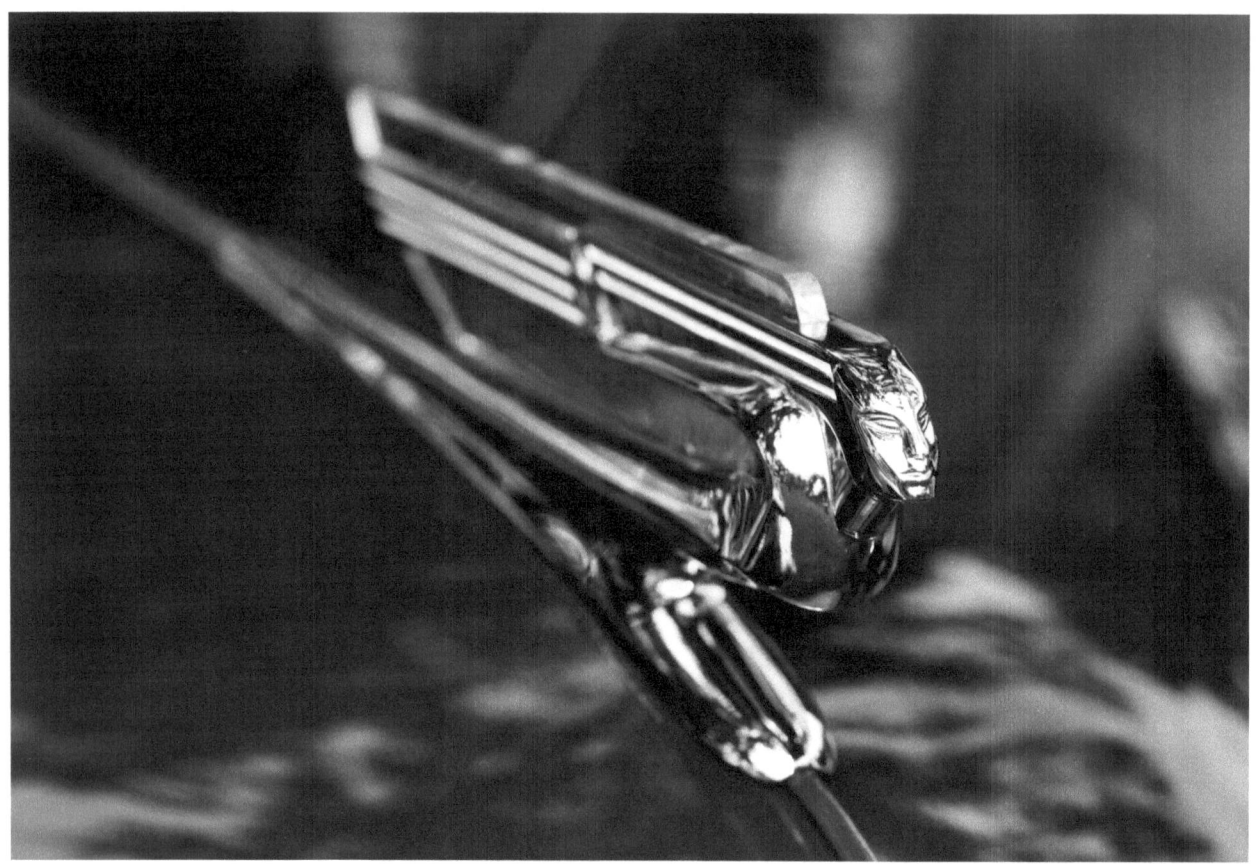

0705

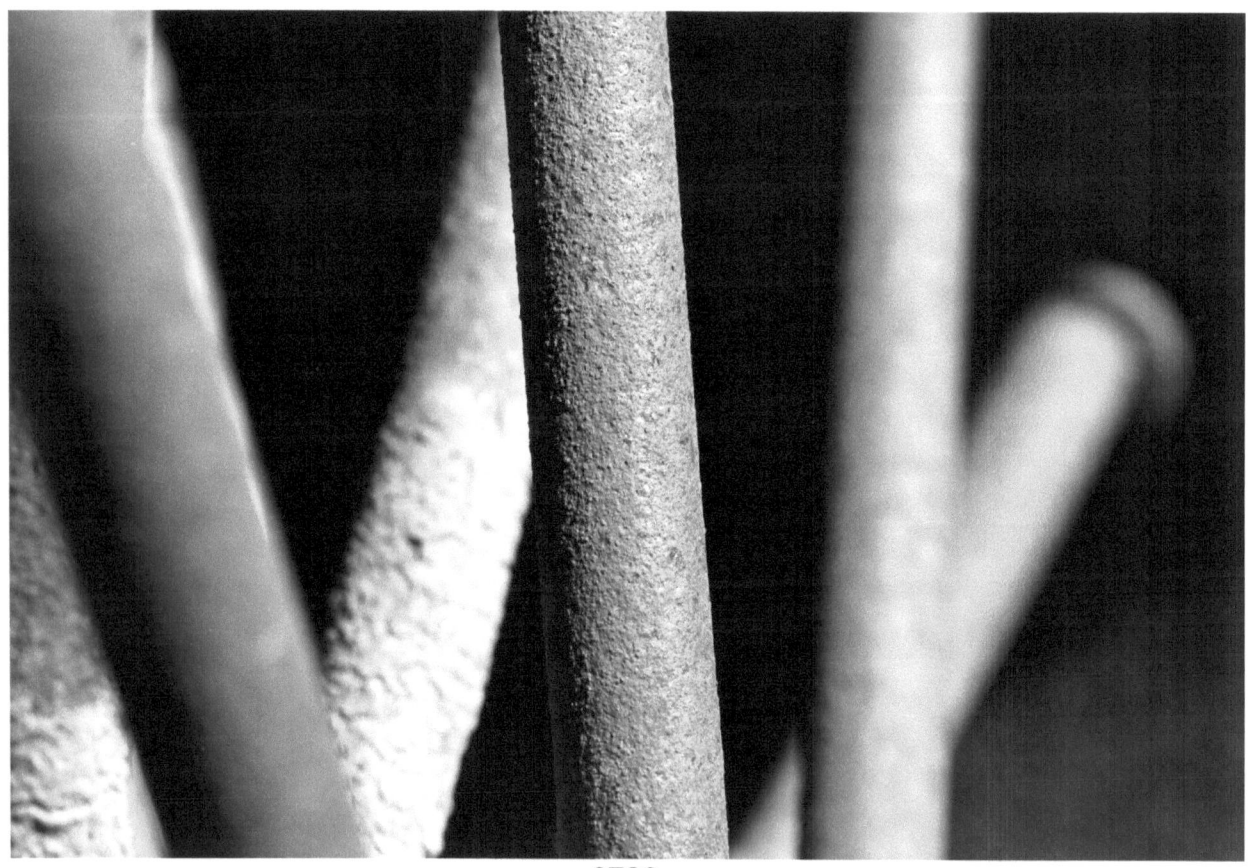

0780

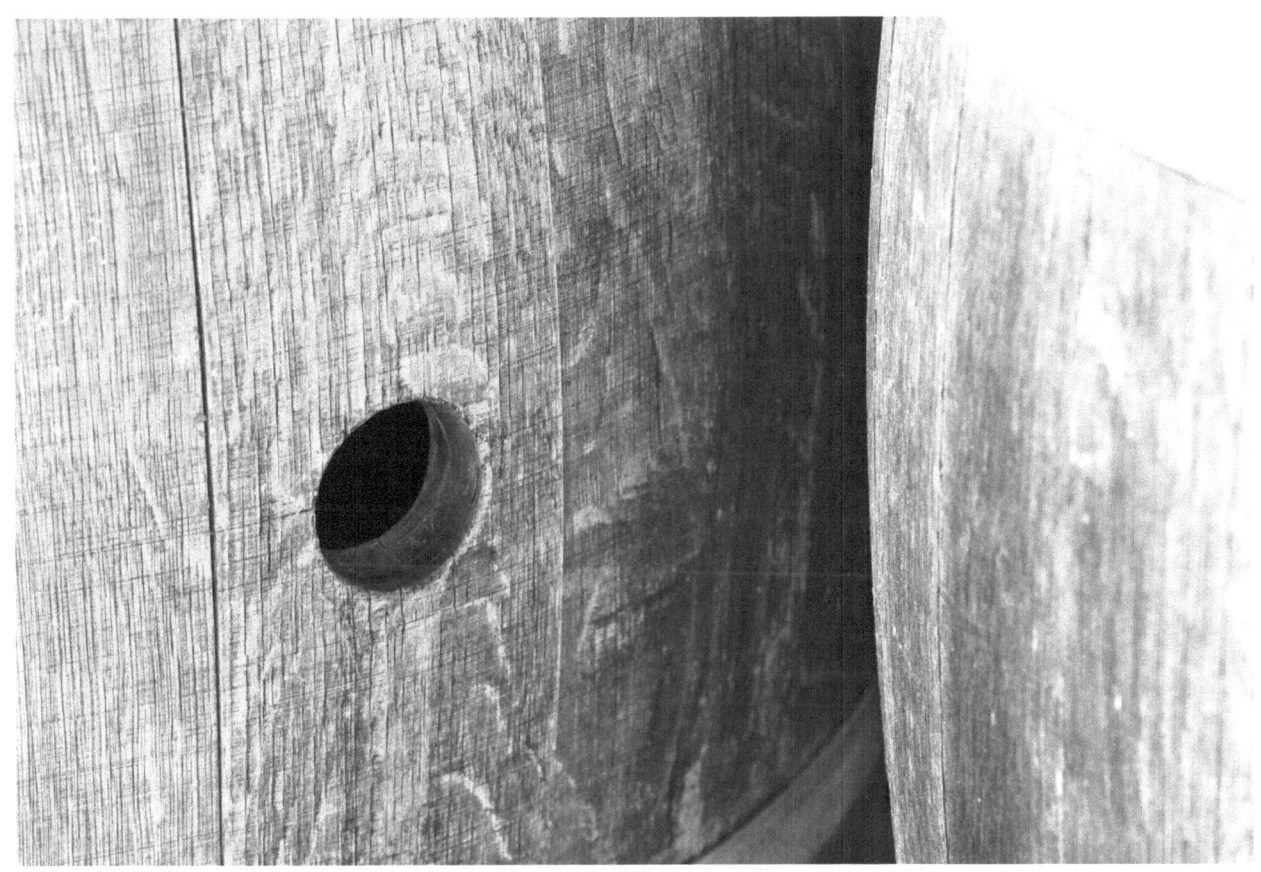

0826

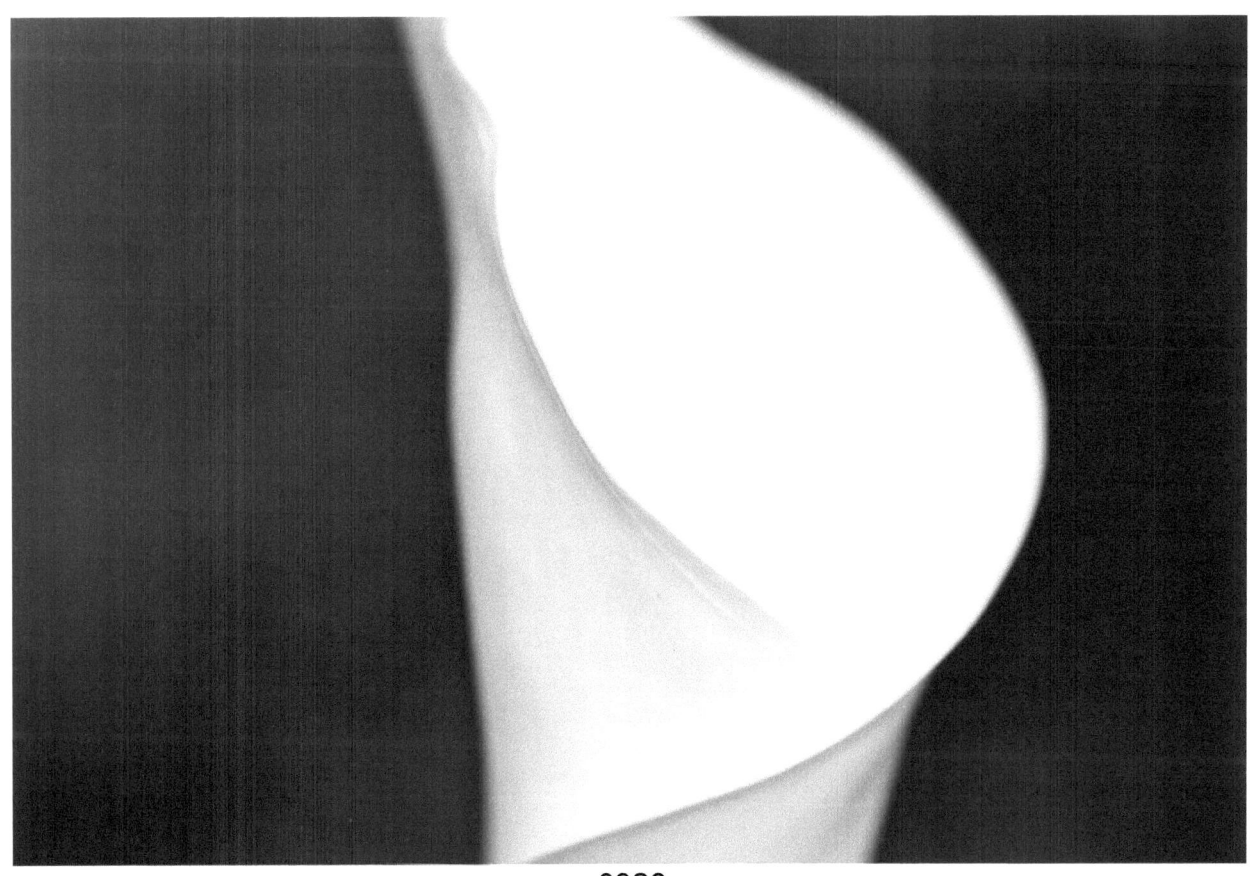

0920

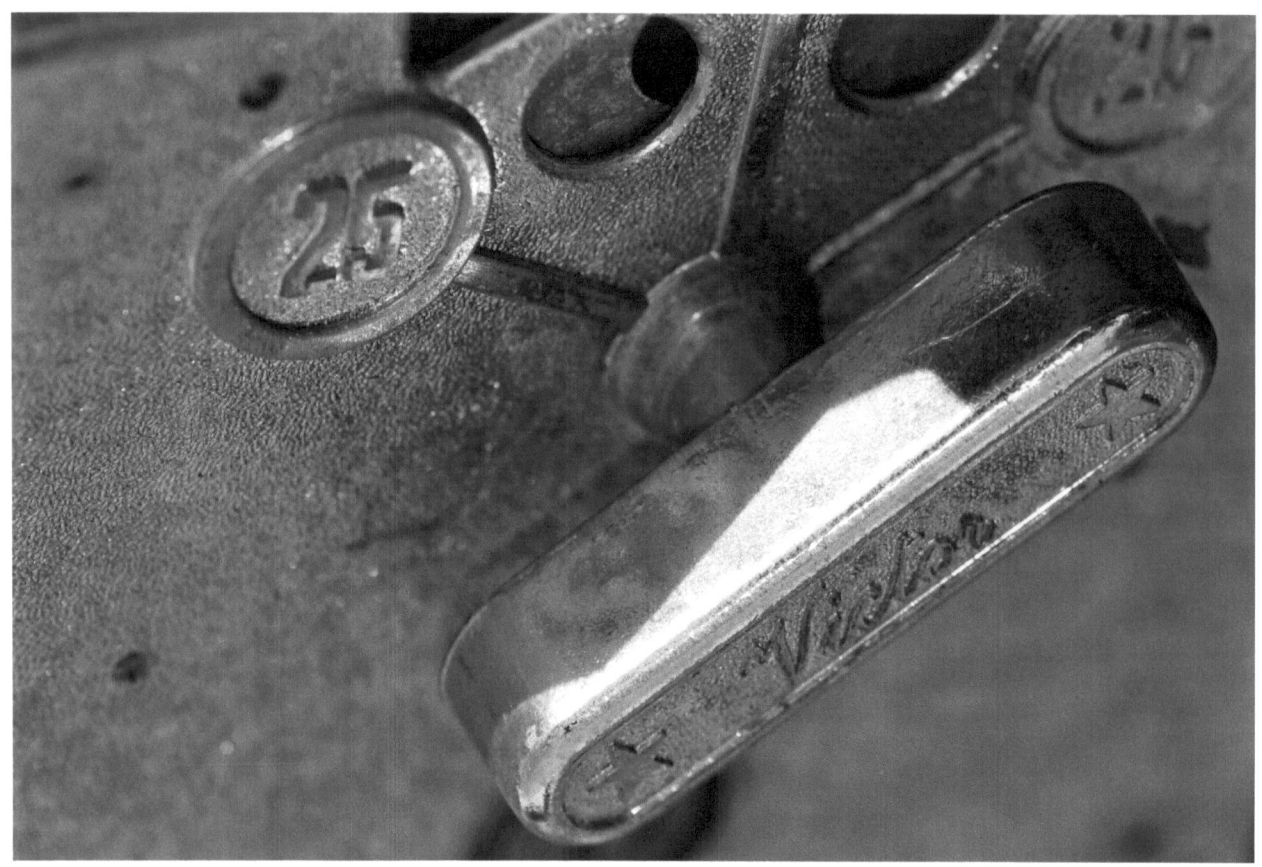

1085

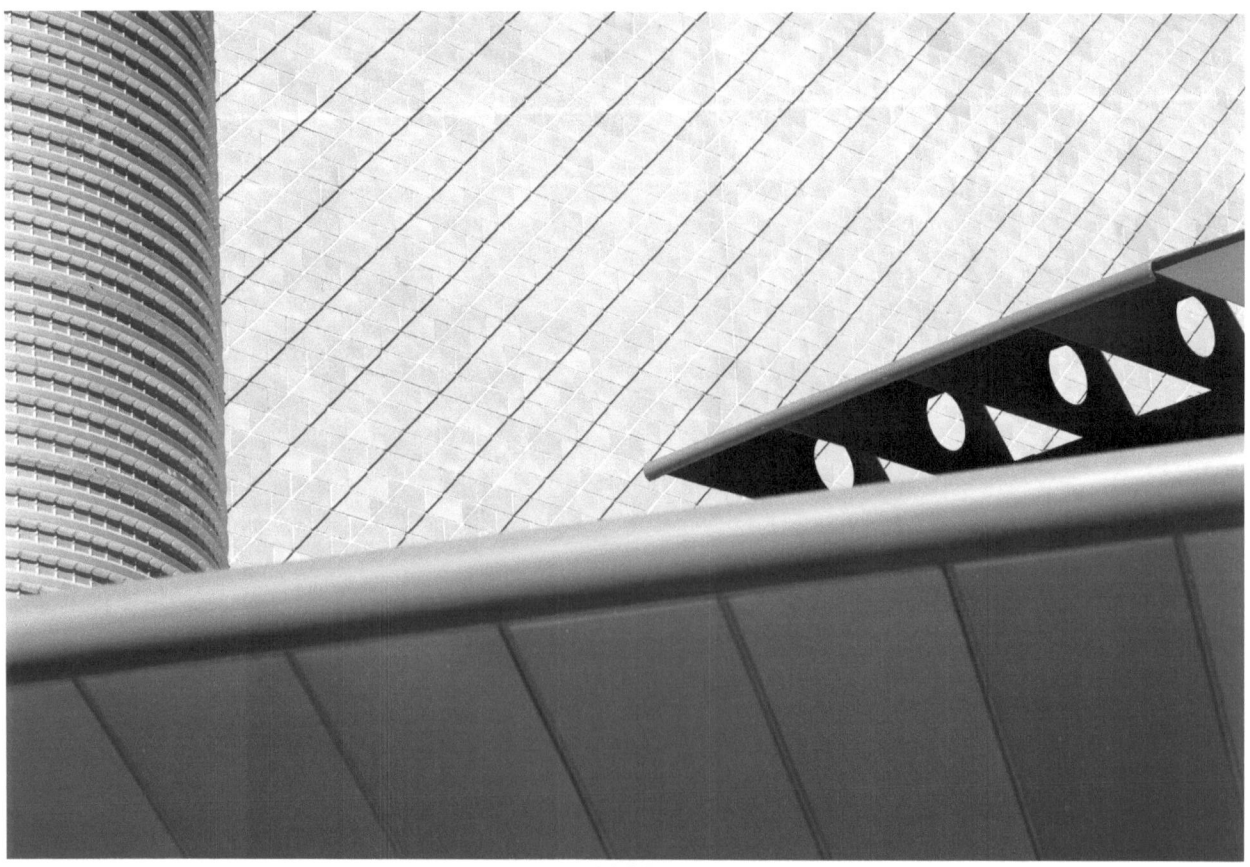

1088

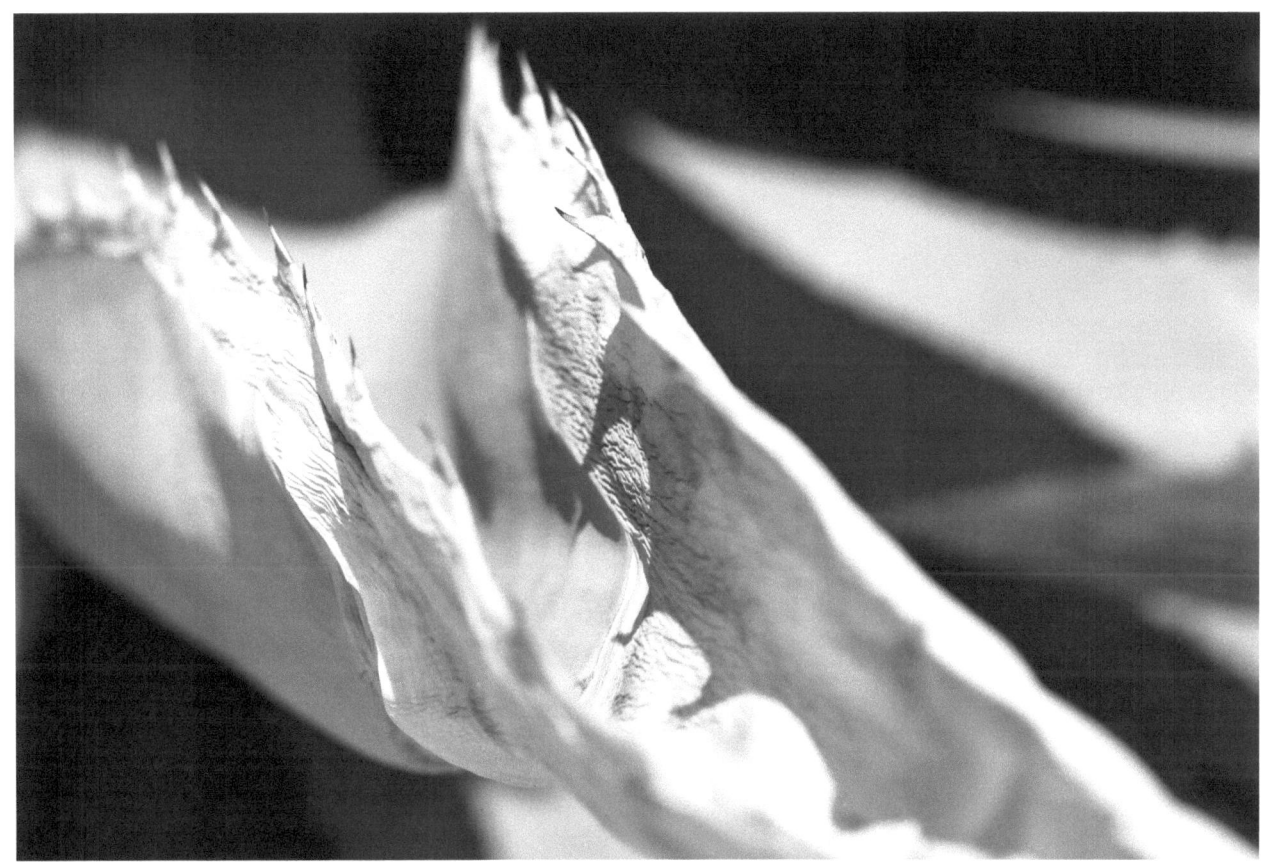

1581

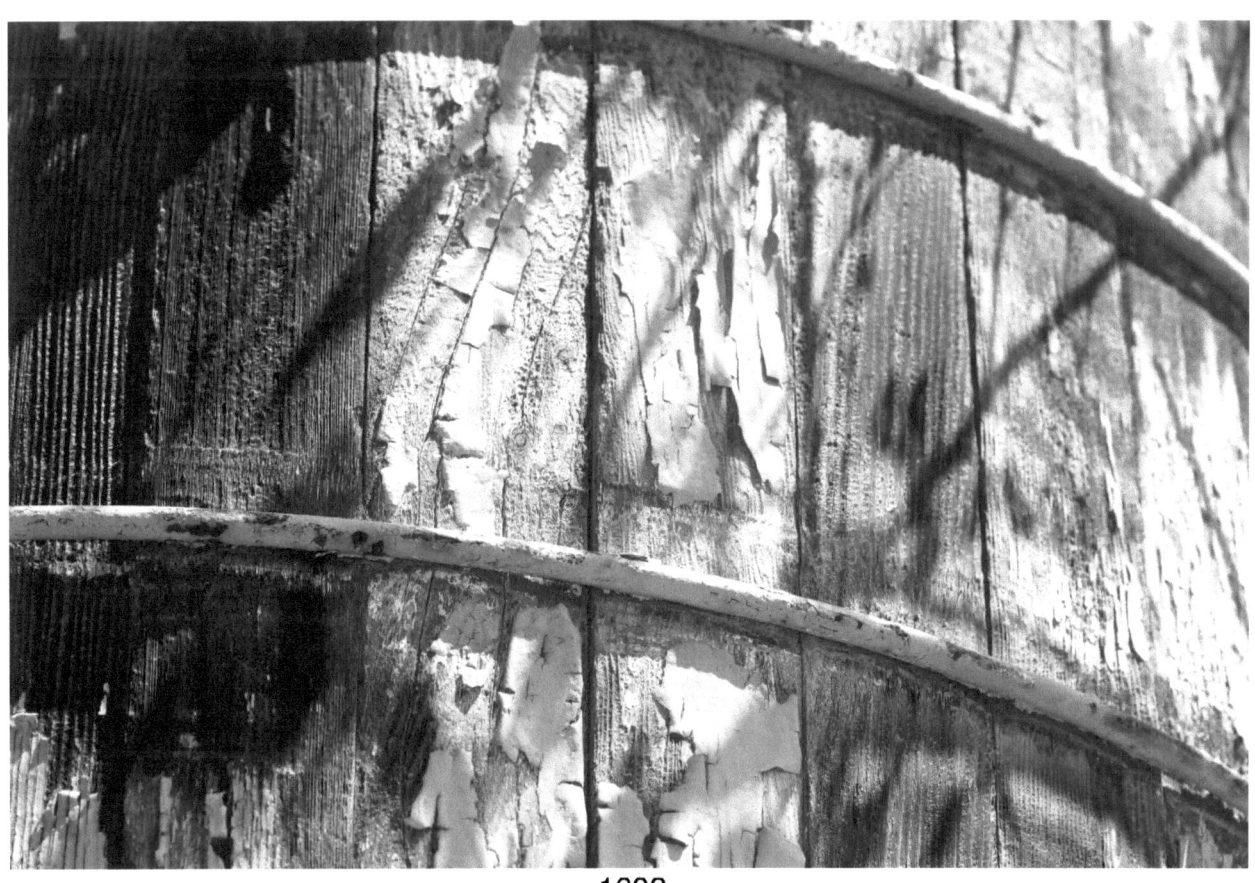

1608

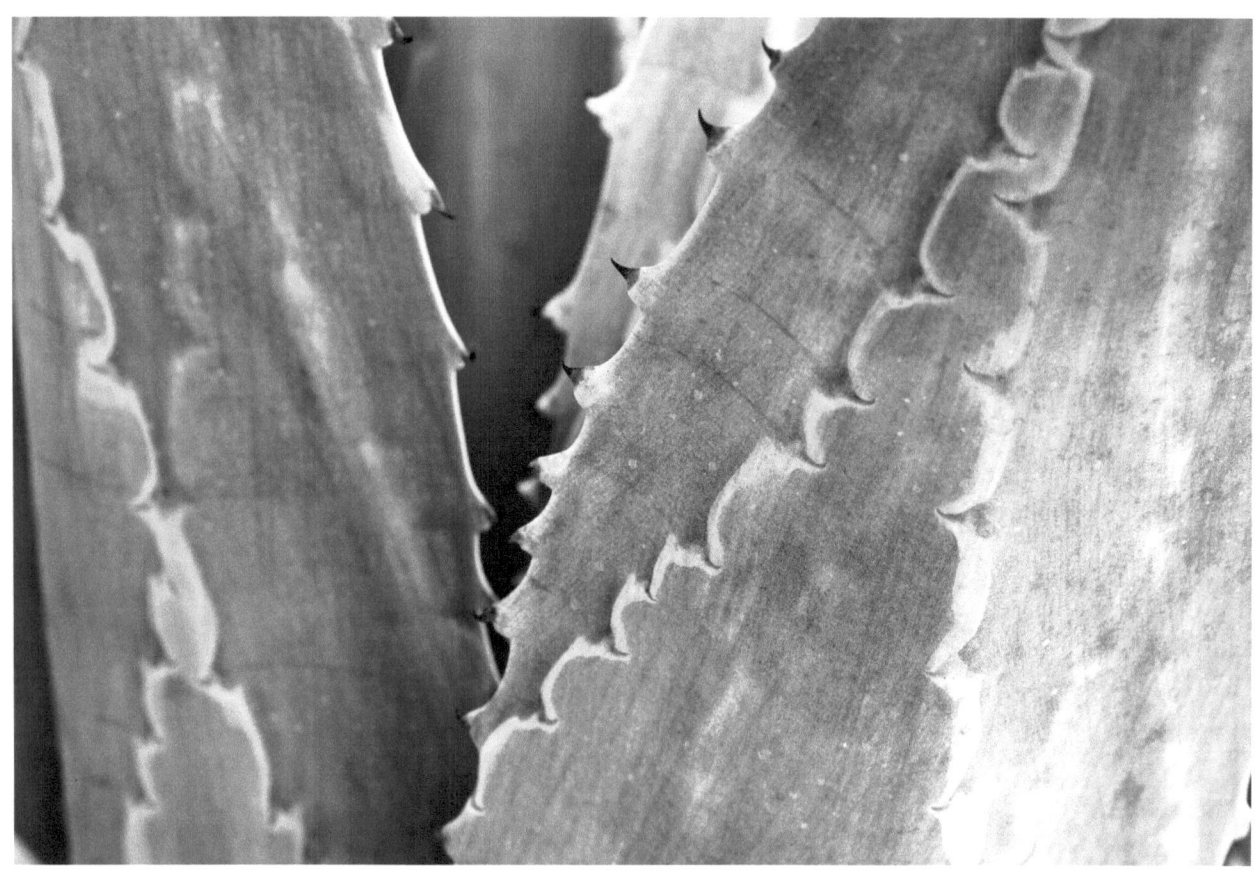

1976

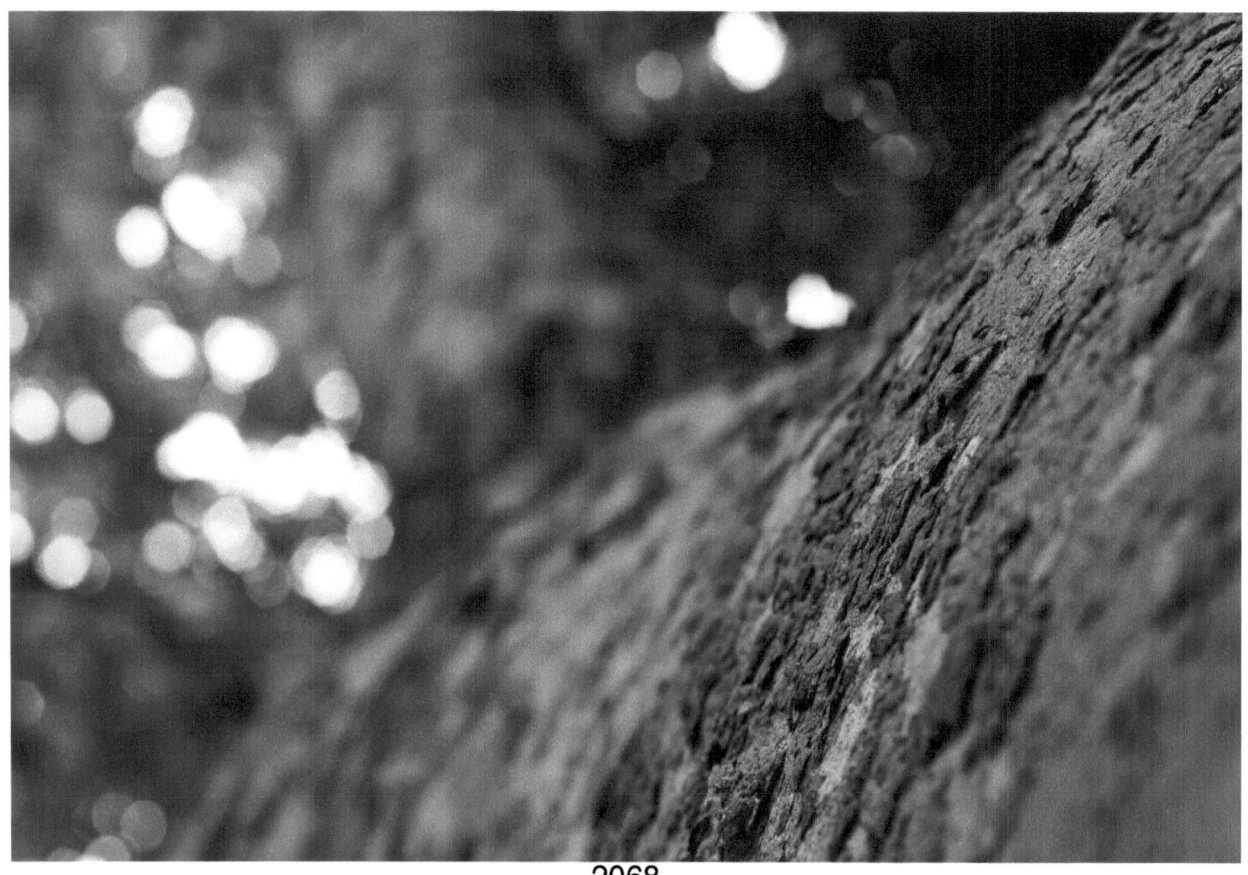

2068

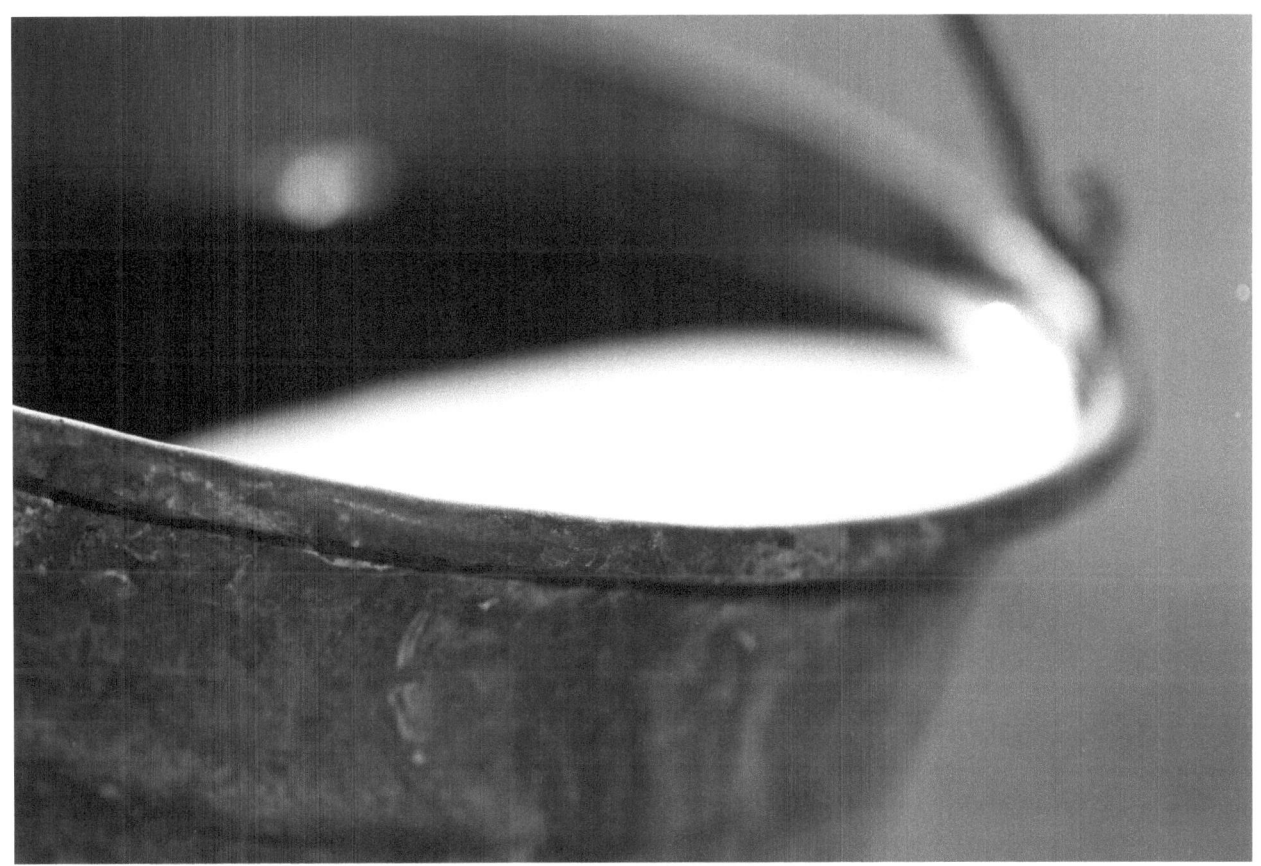

2180

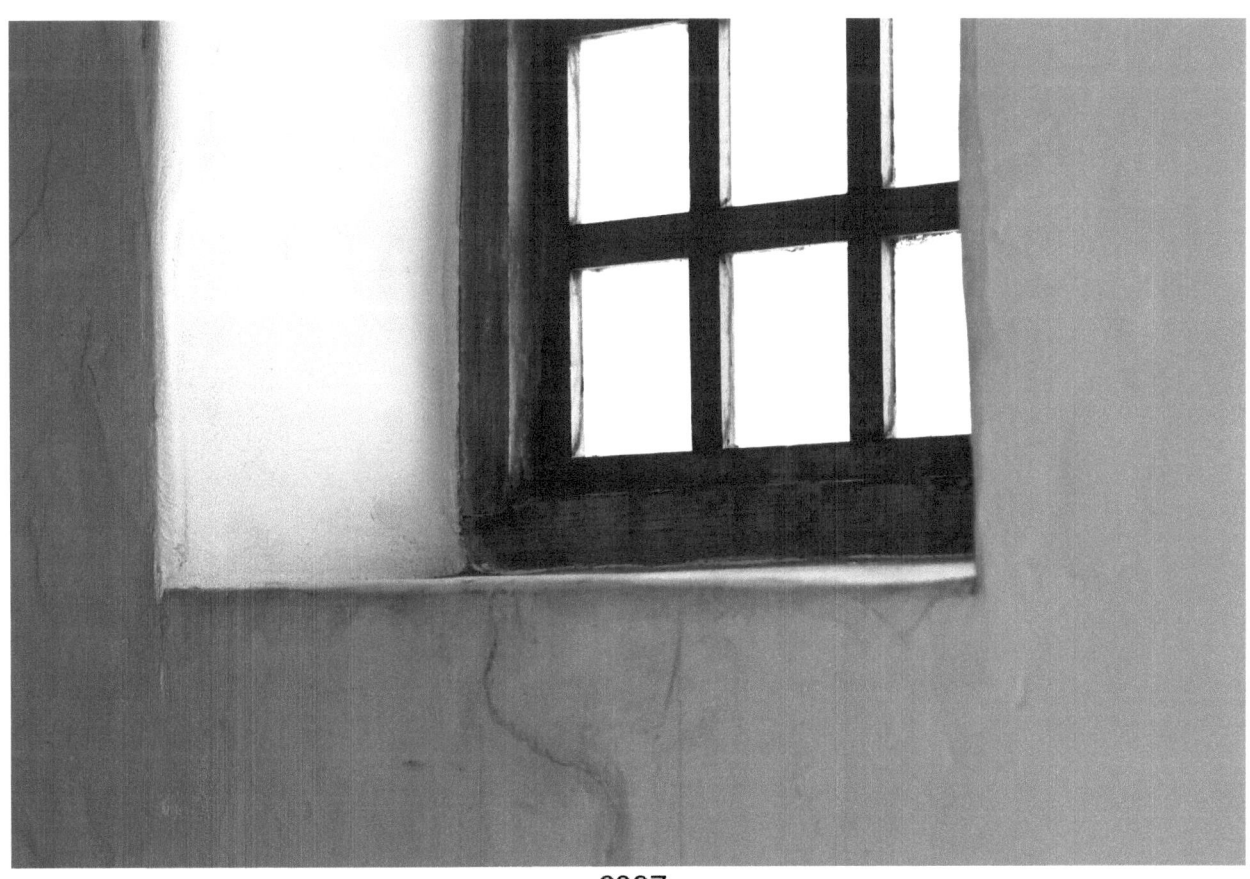

2397

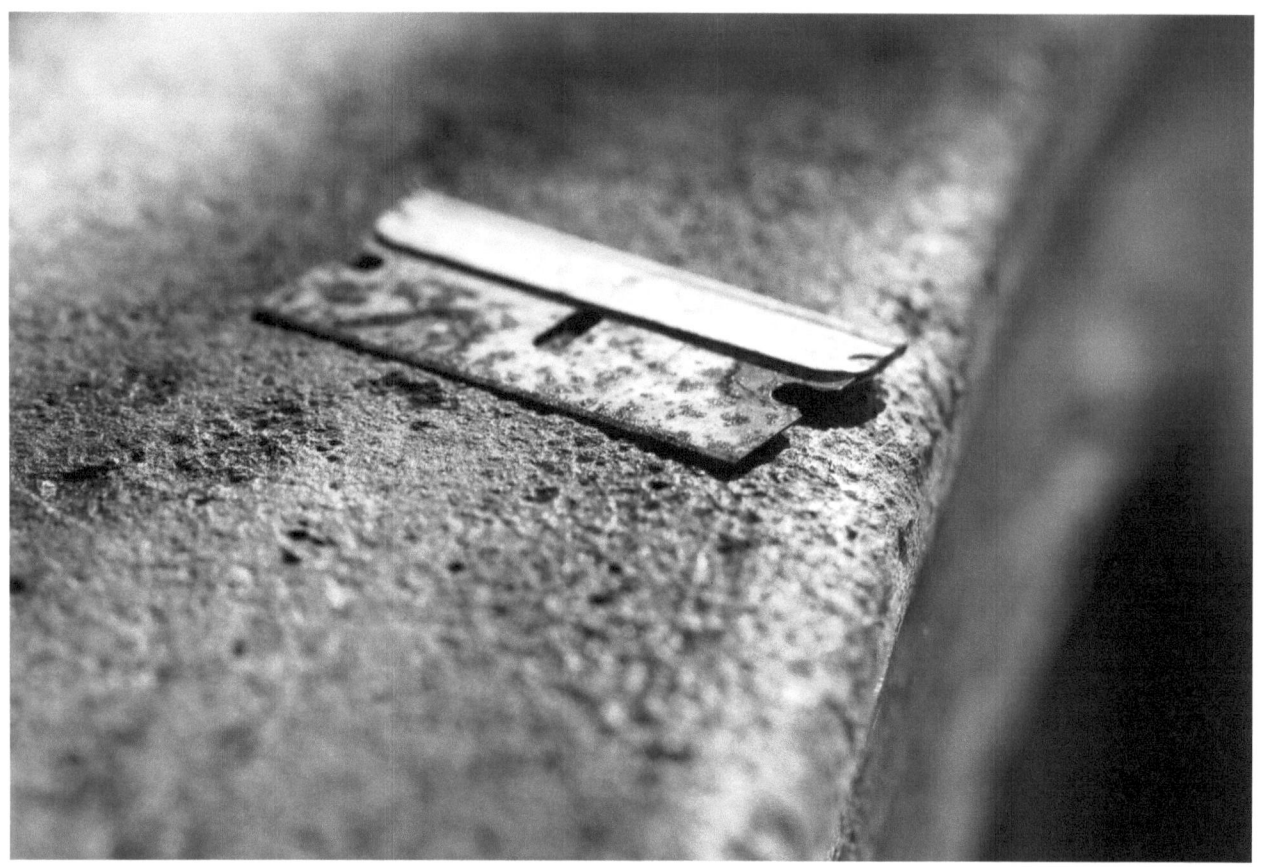

2467

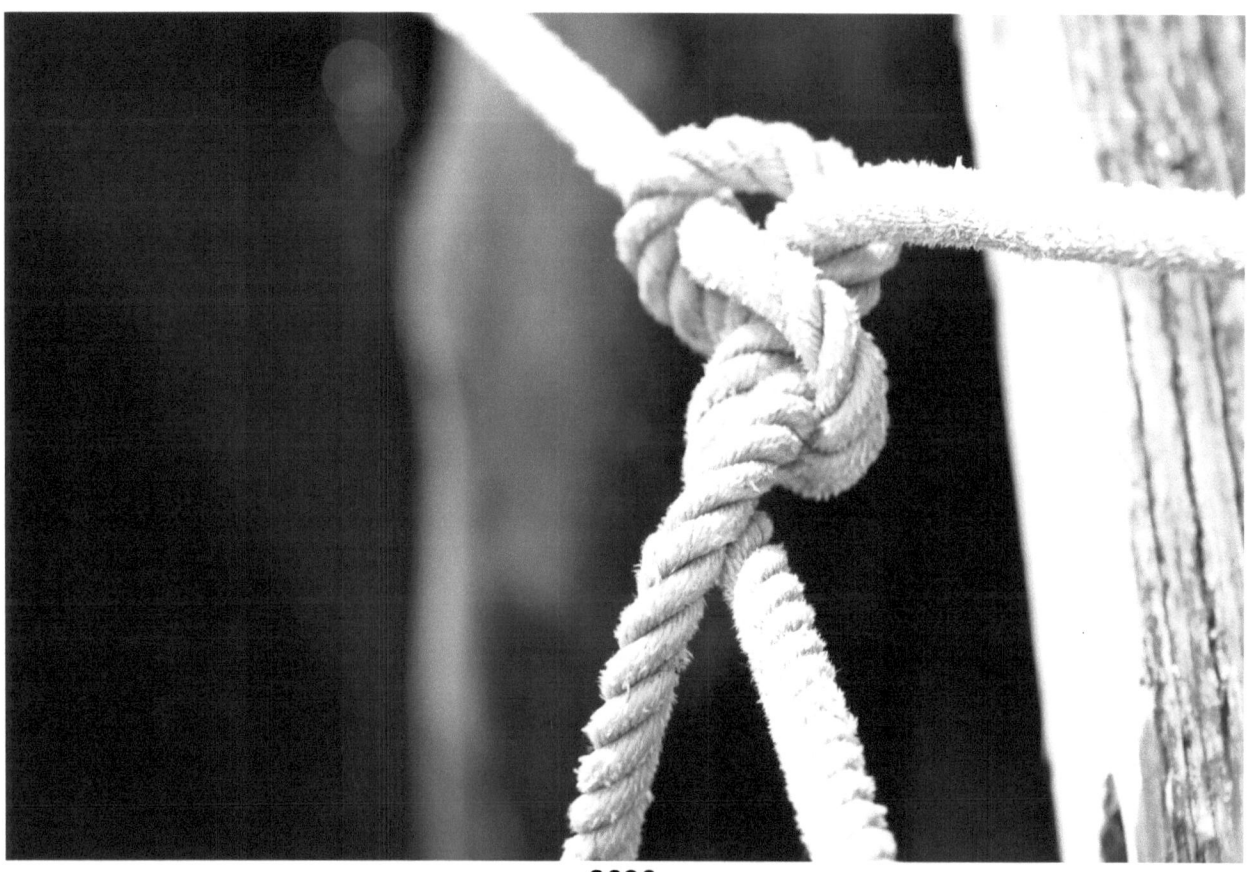

2686

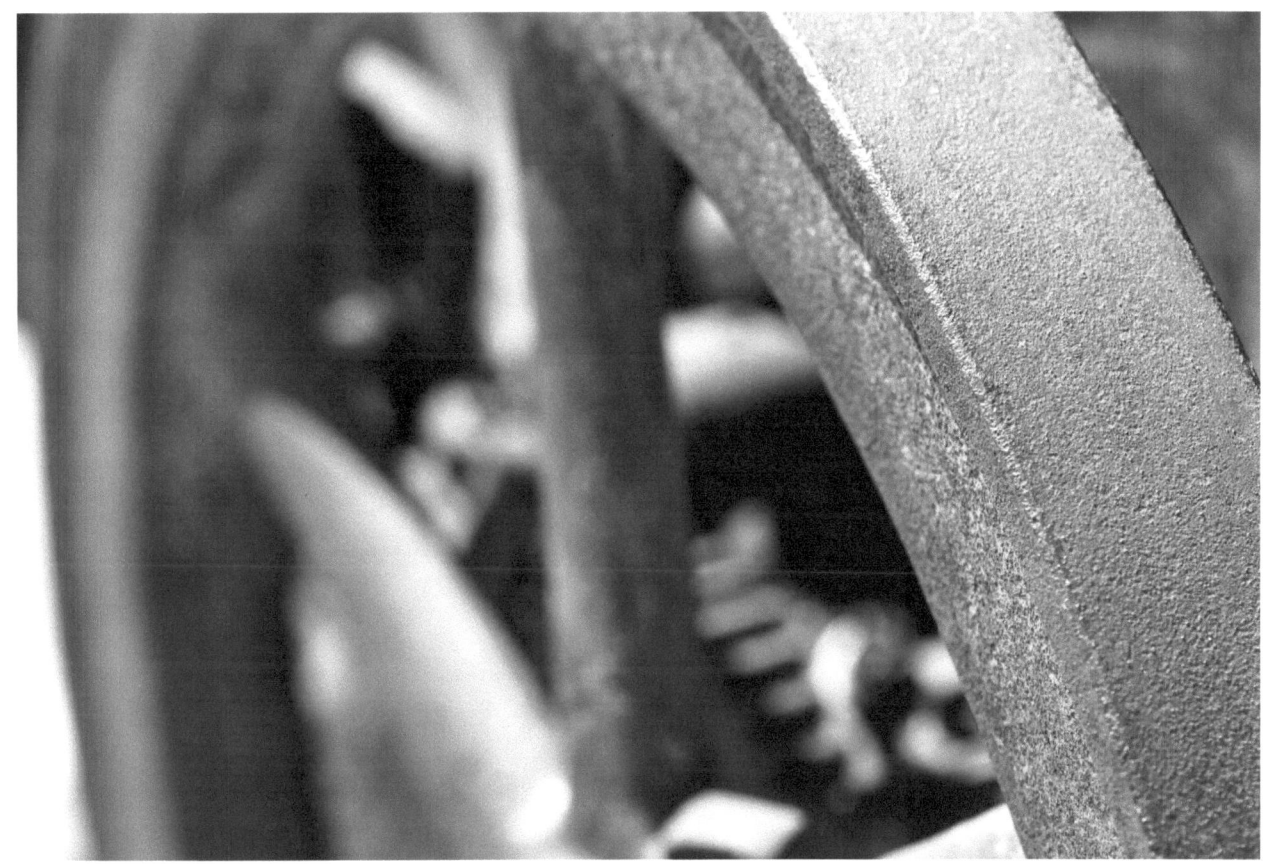

2962

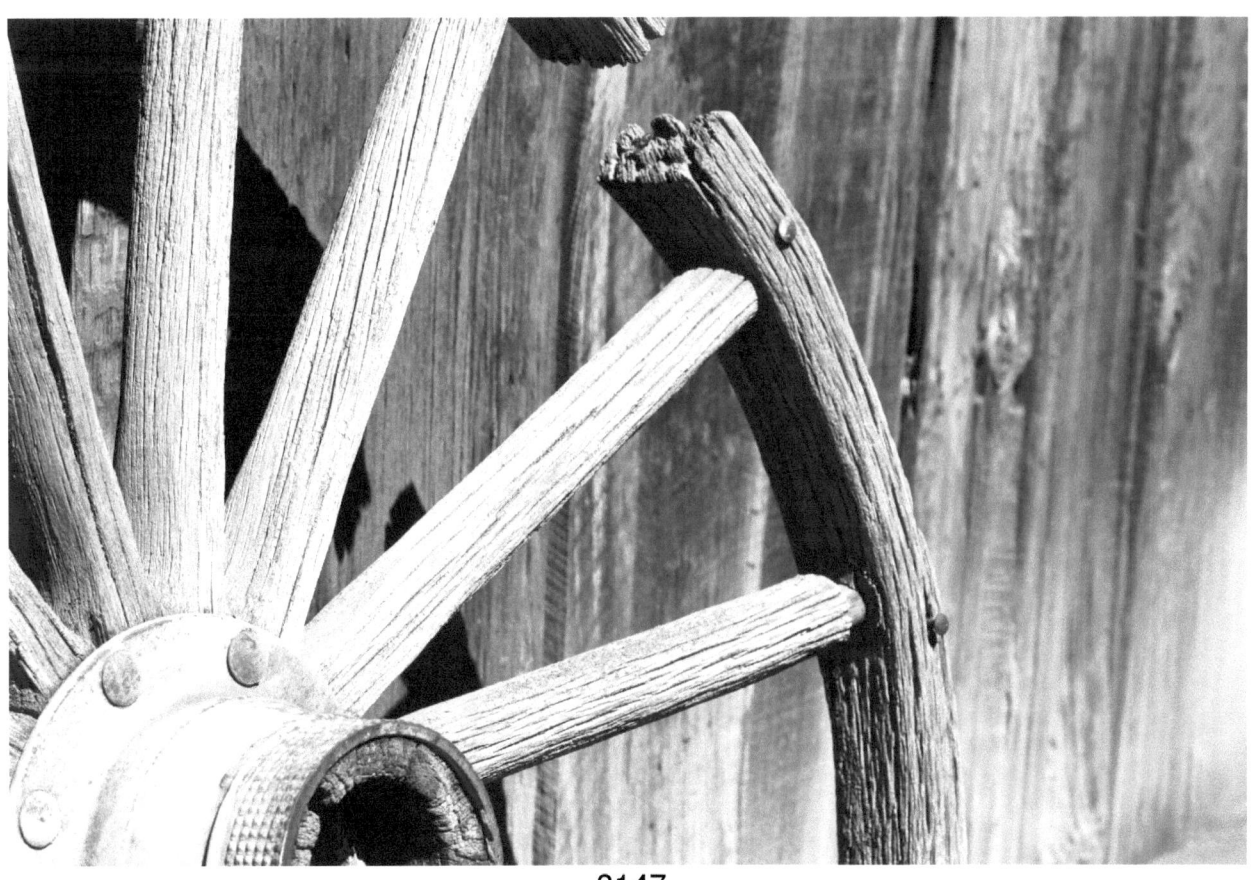

3147

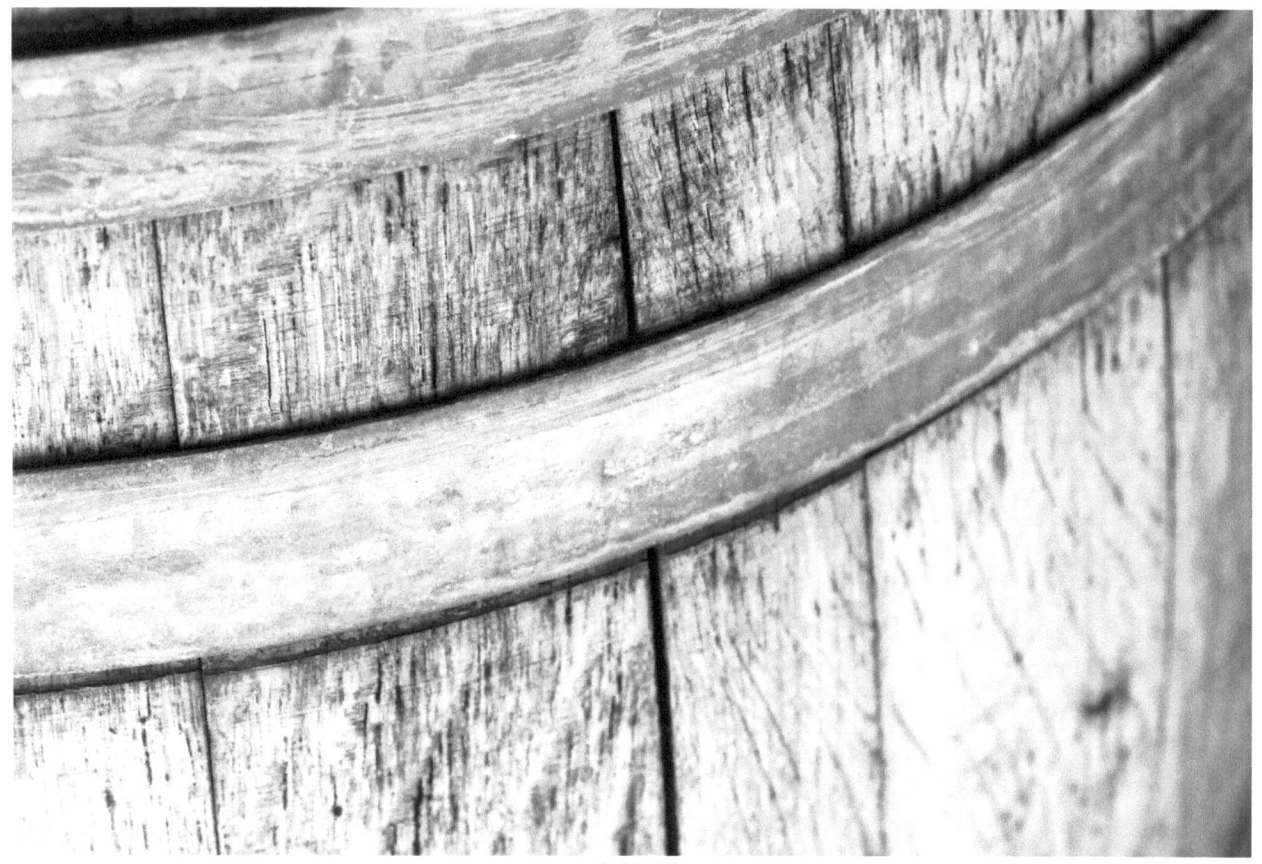

3151

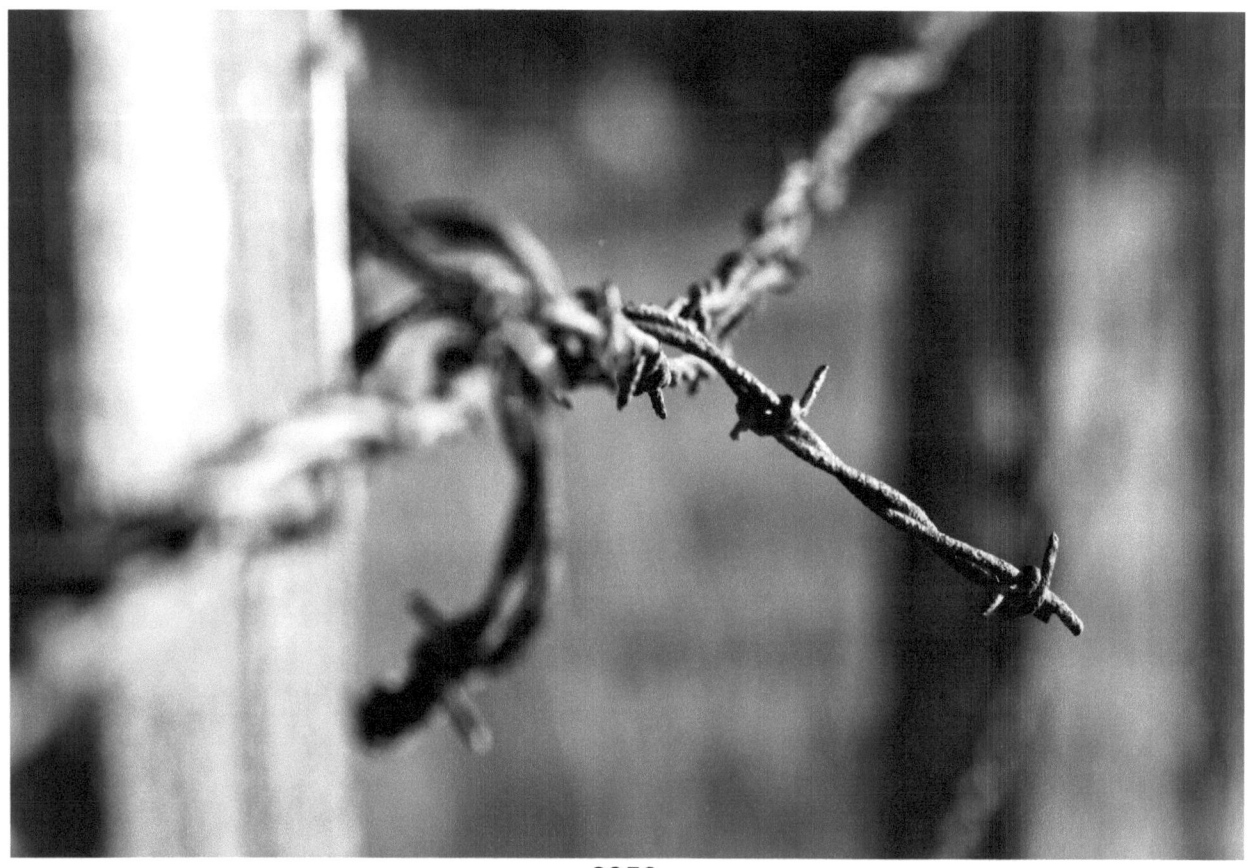

3359

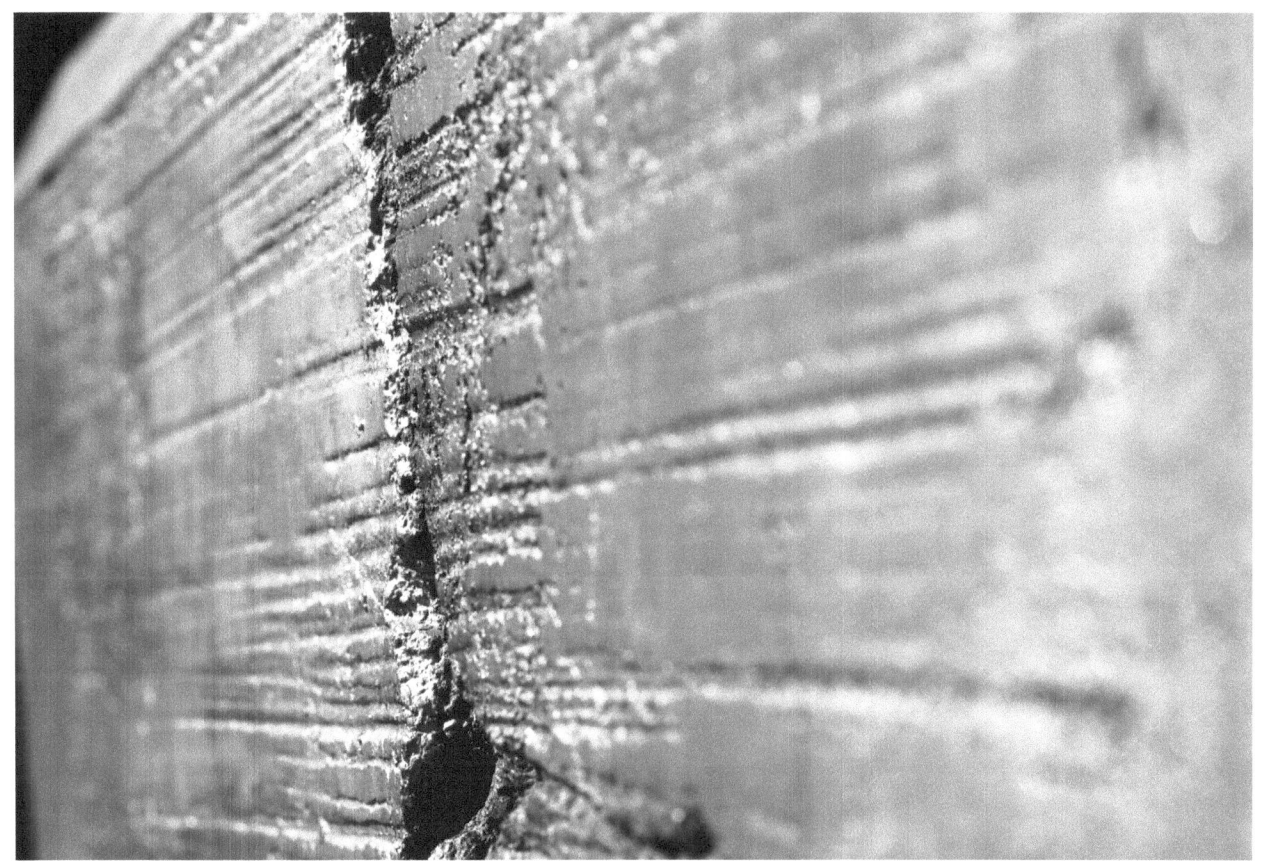

3656

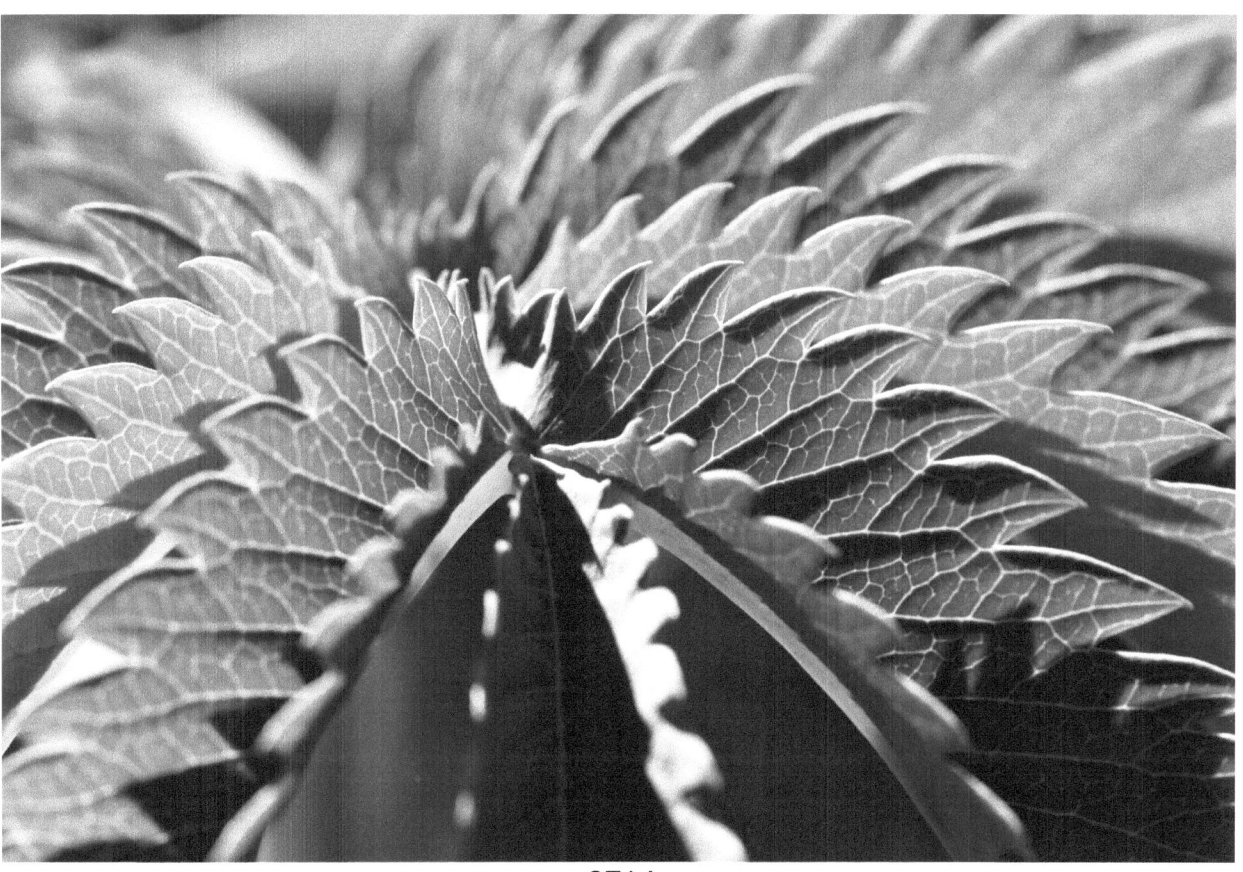

3714

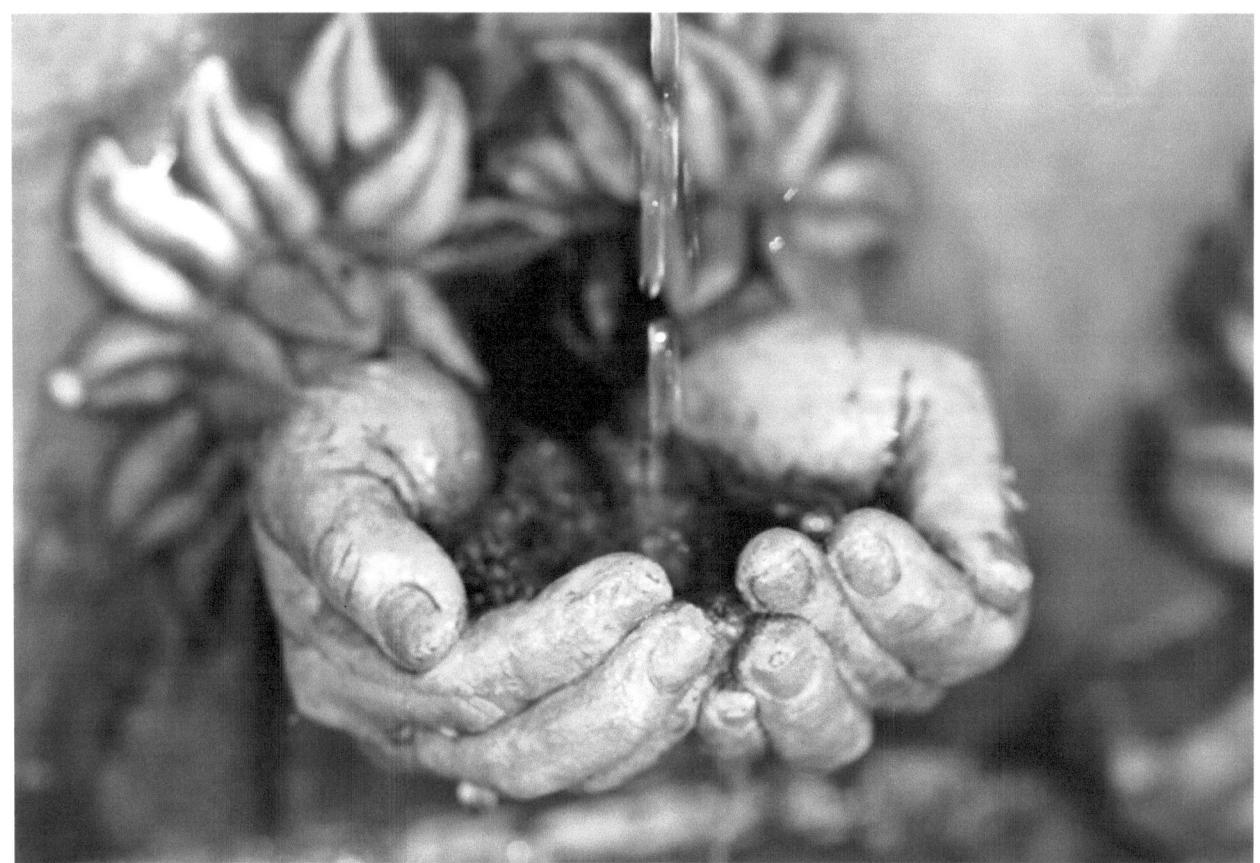

3720

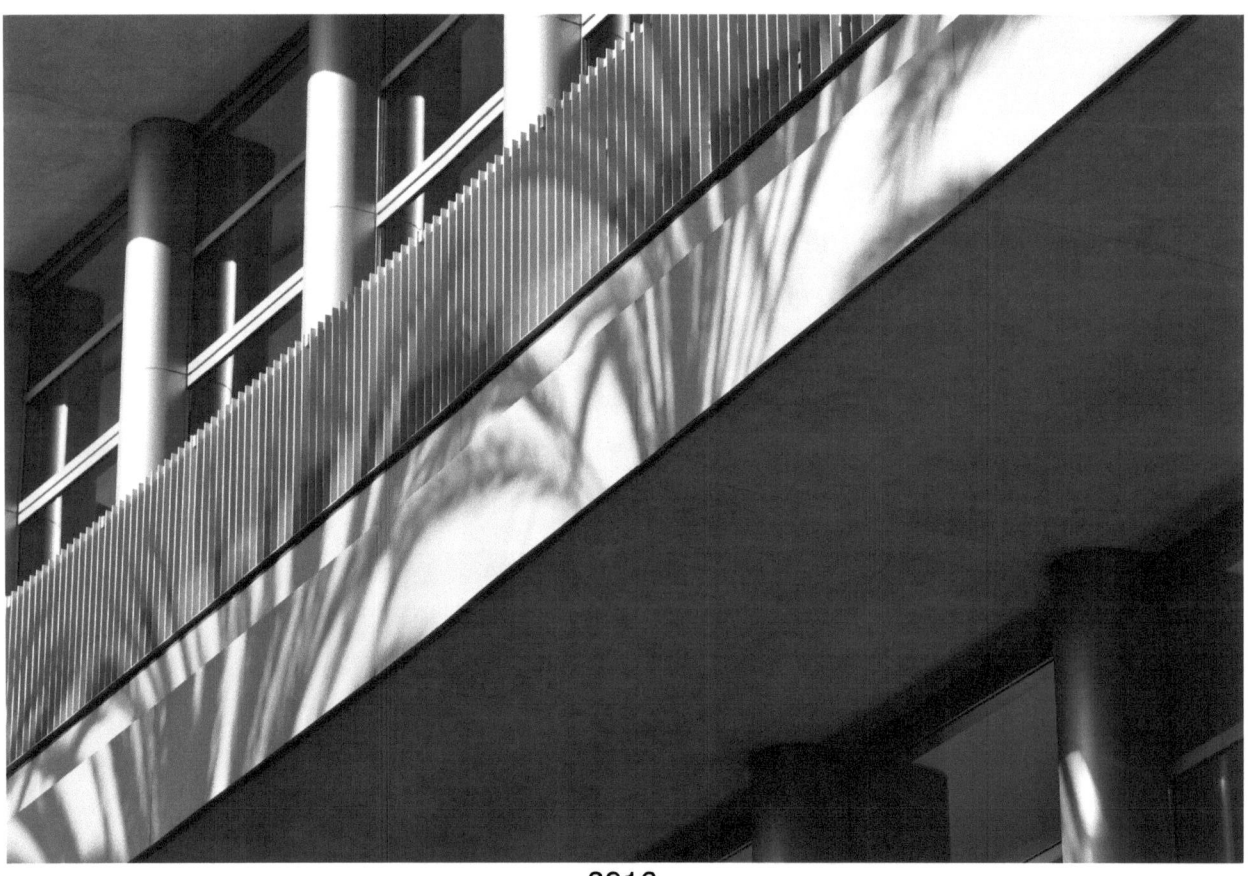

3916

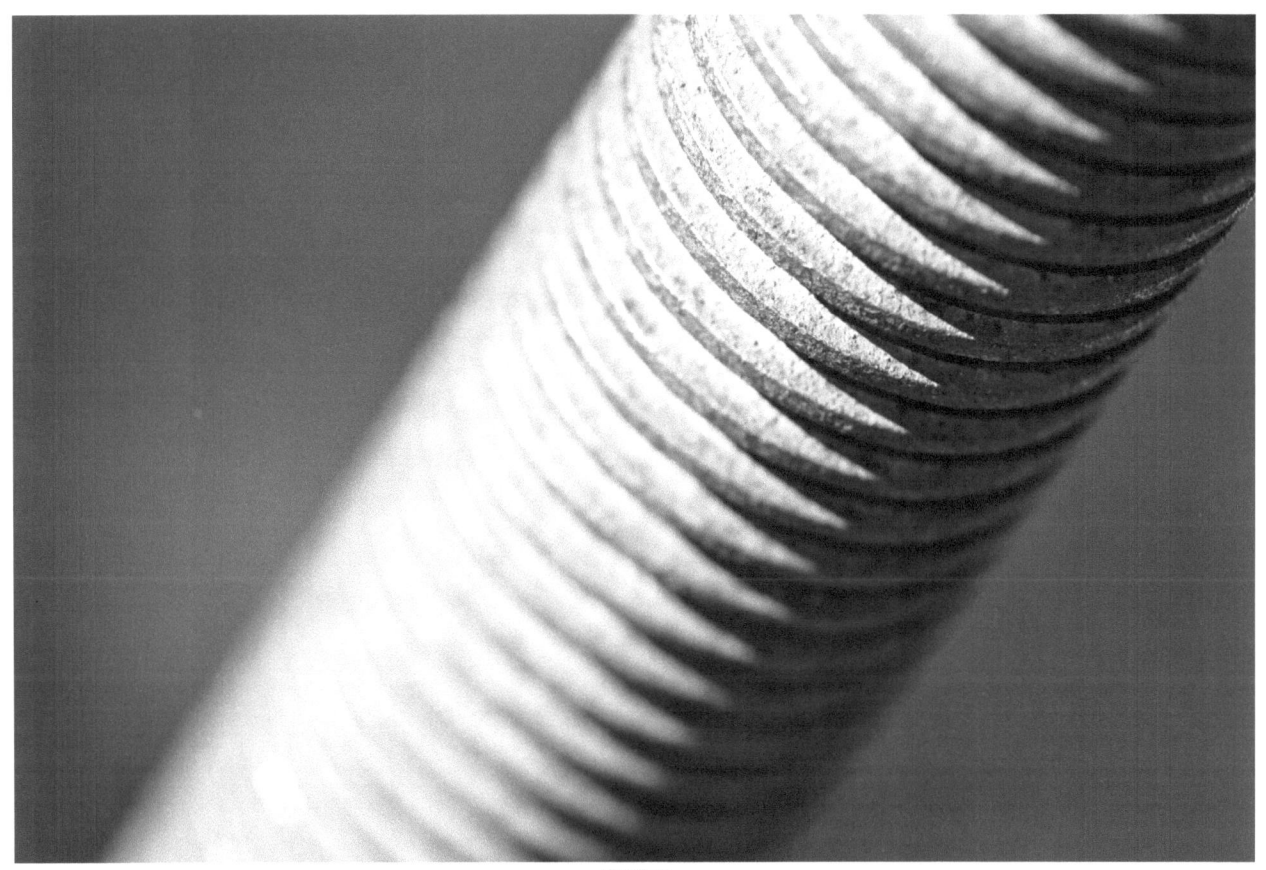

3937

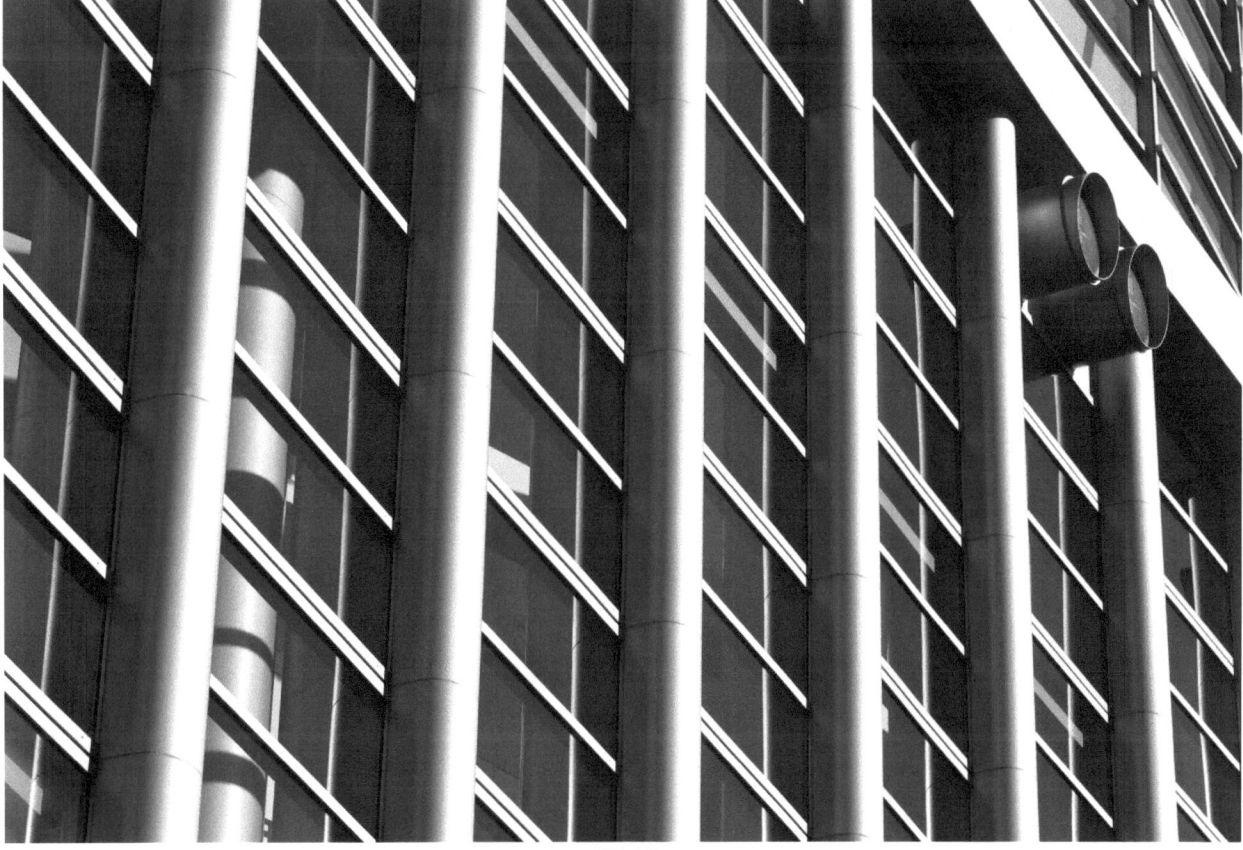

3943

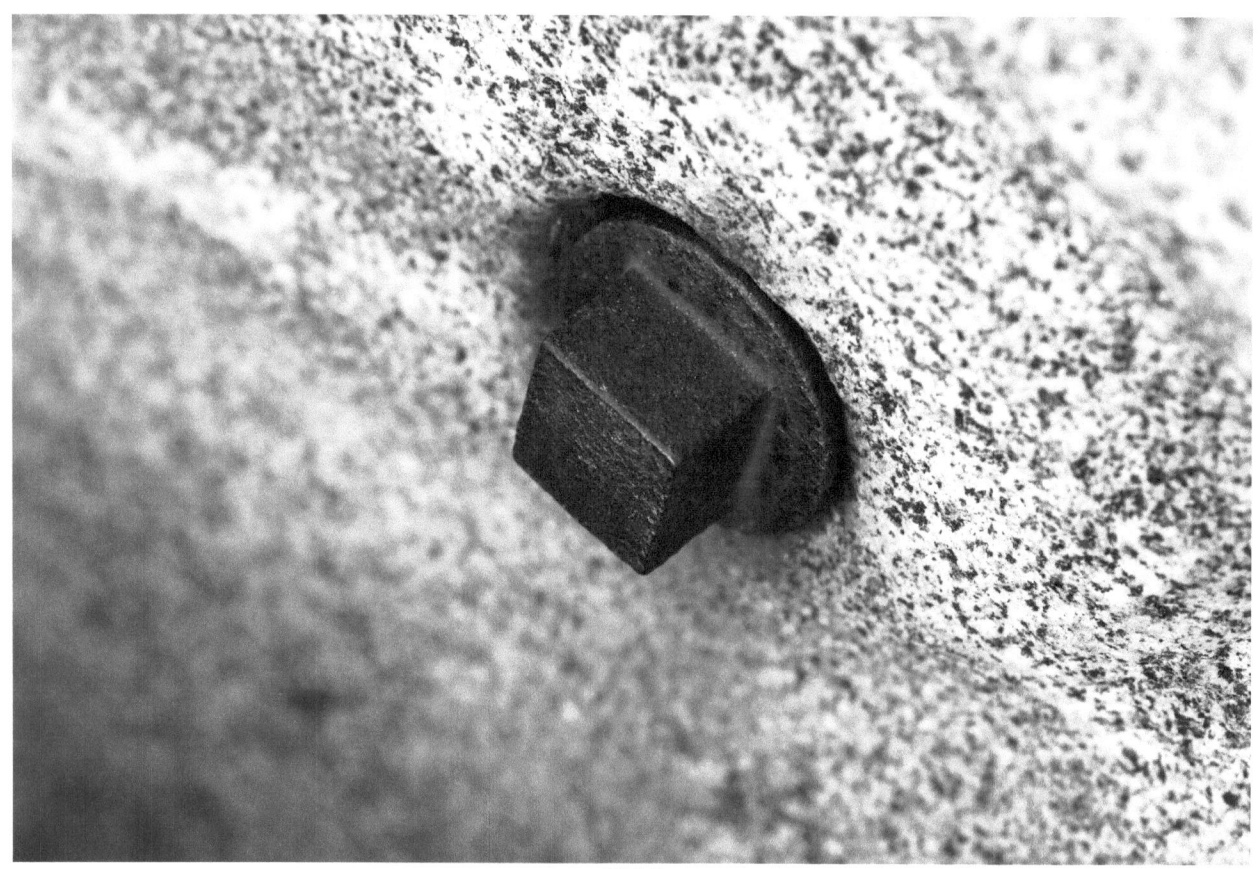

4035

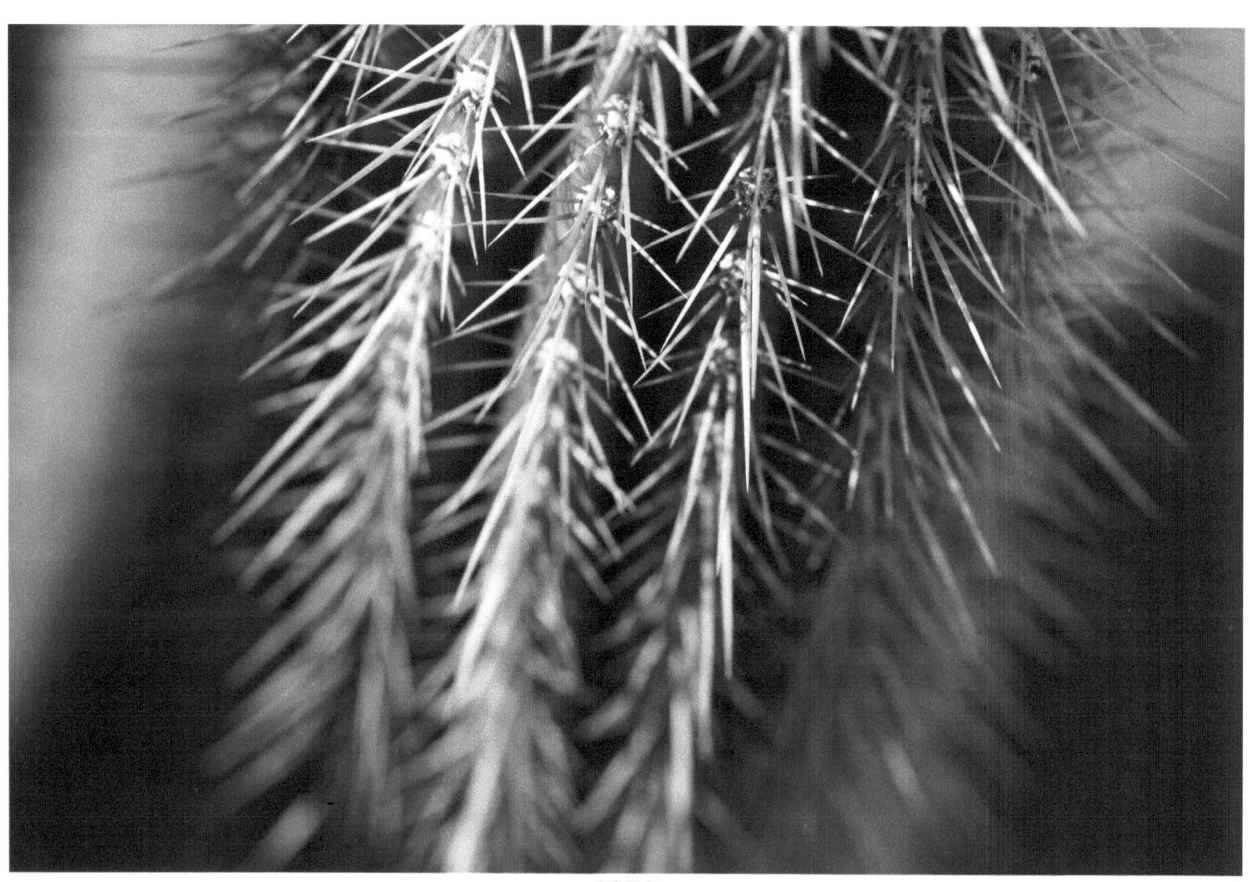

4070

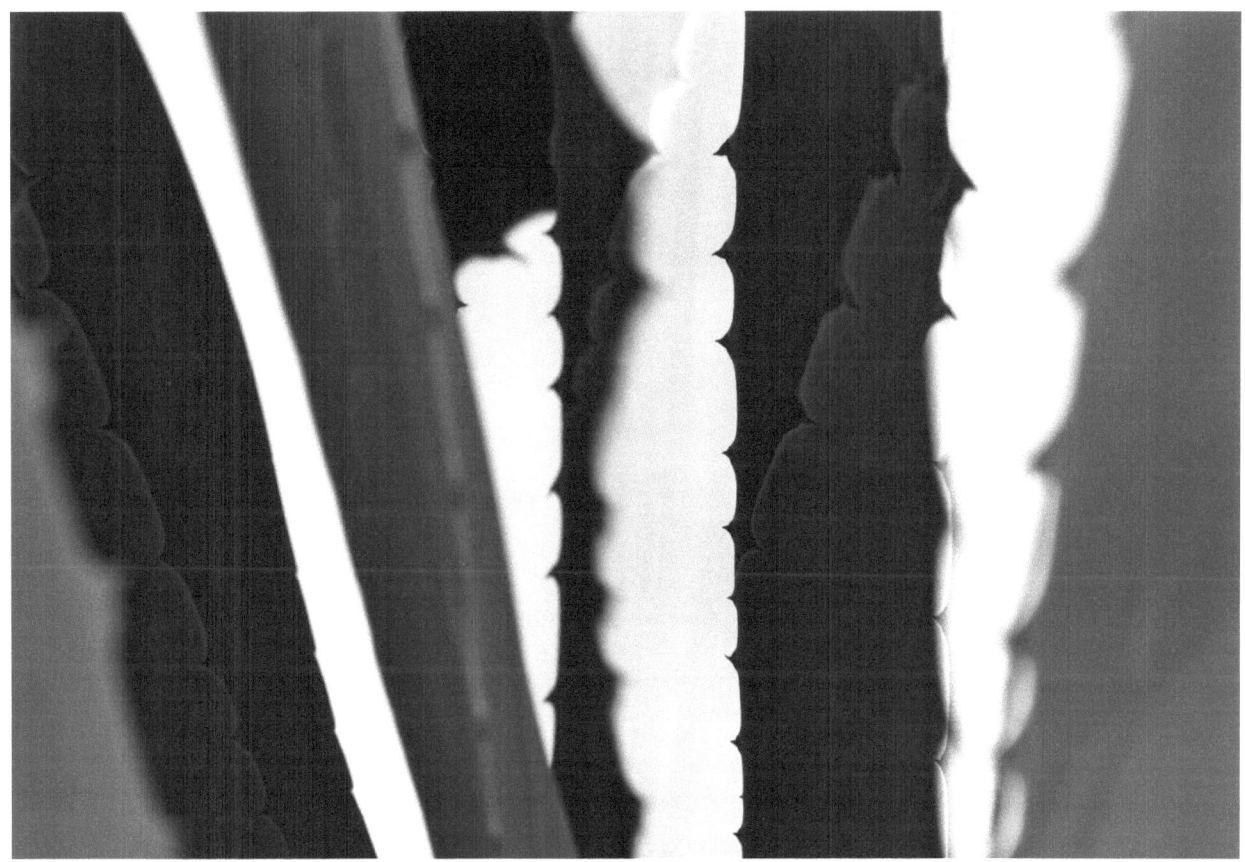

4099

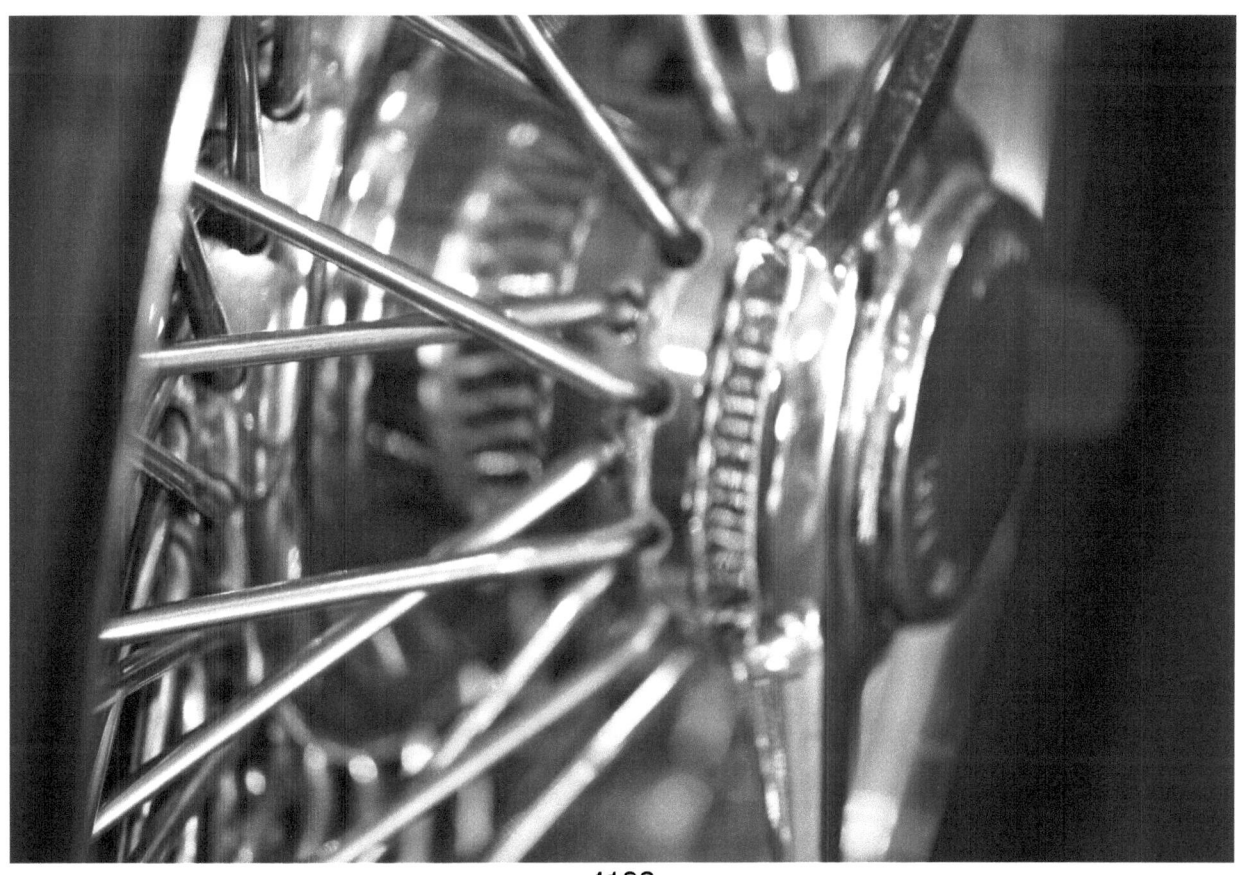

4193

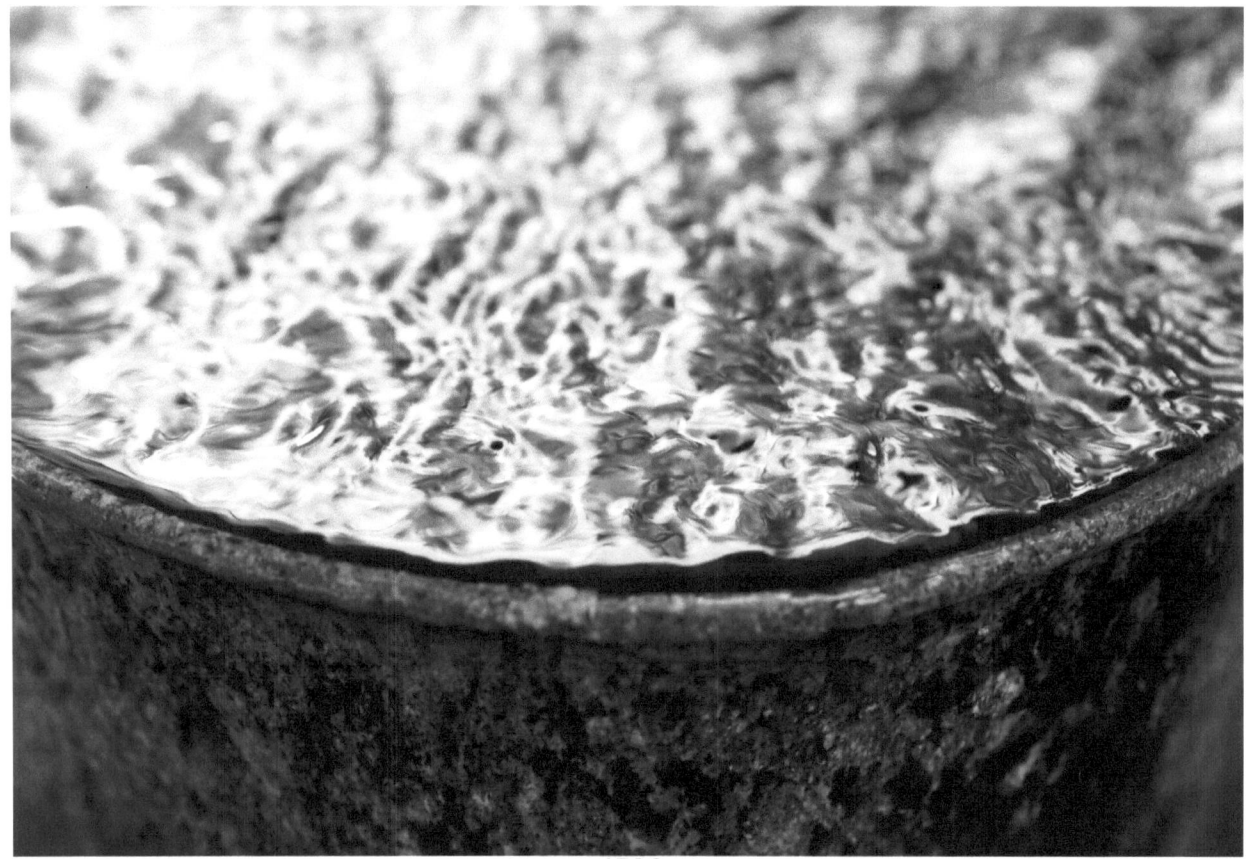

4533

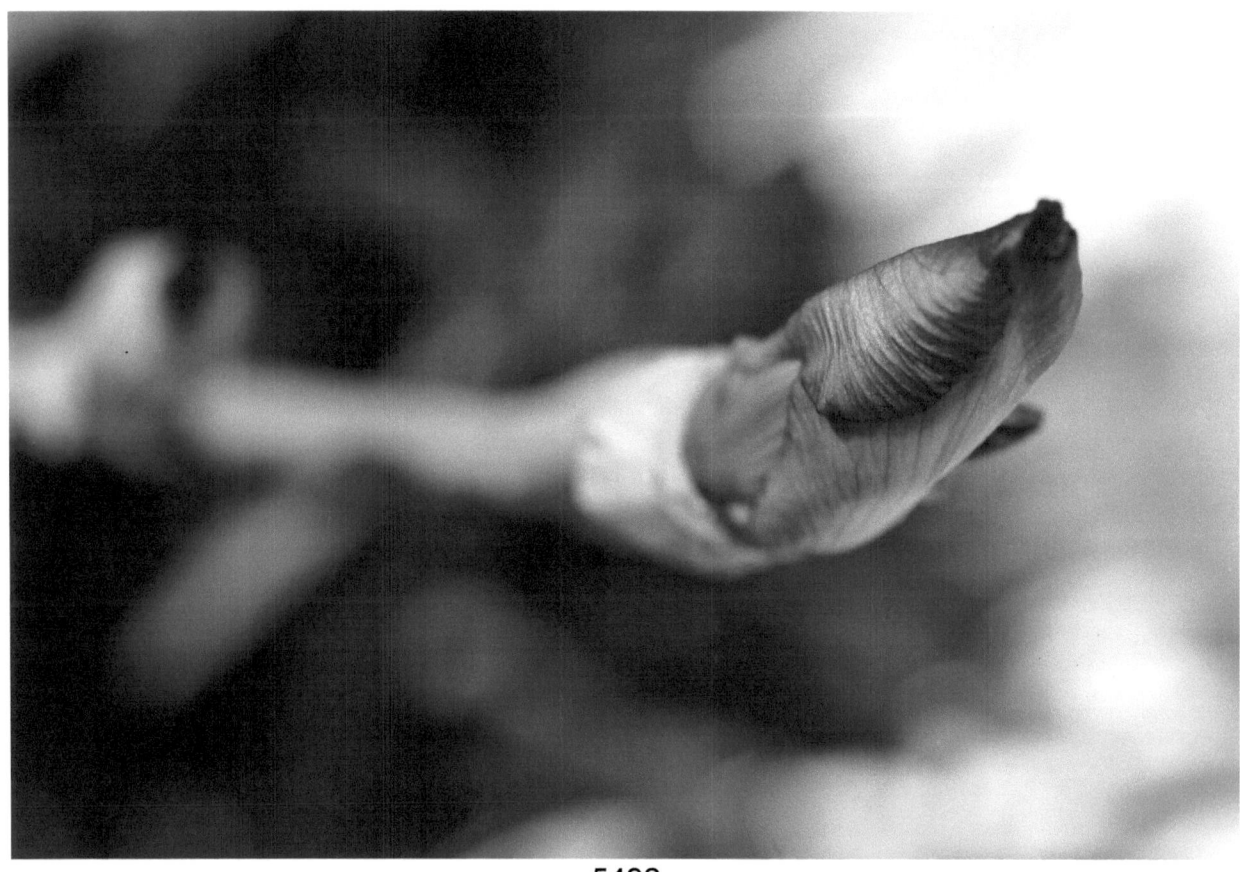

5492

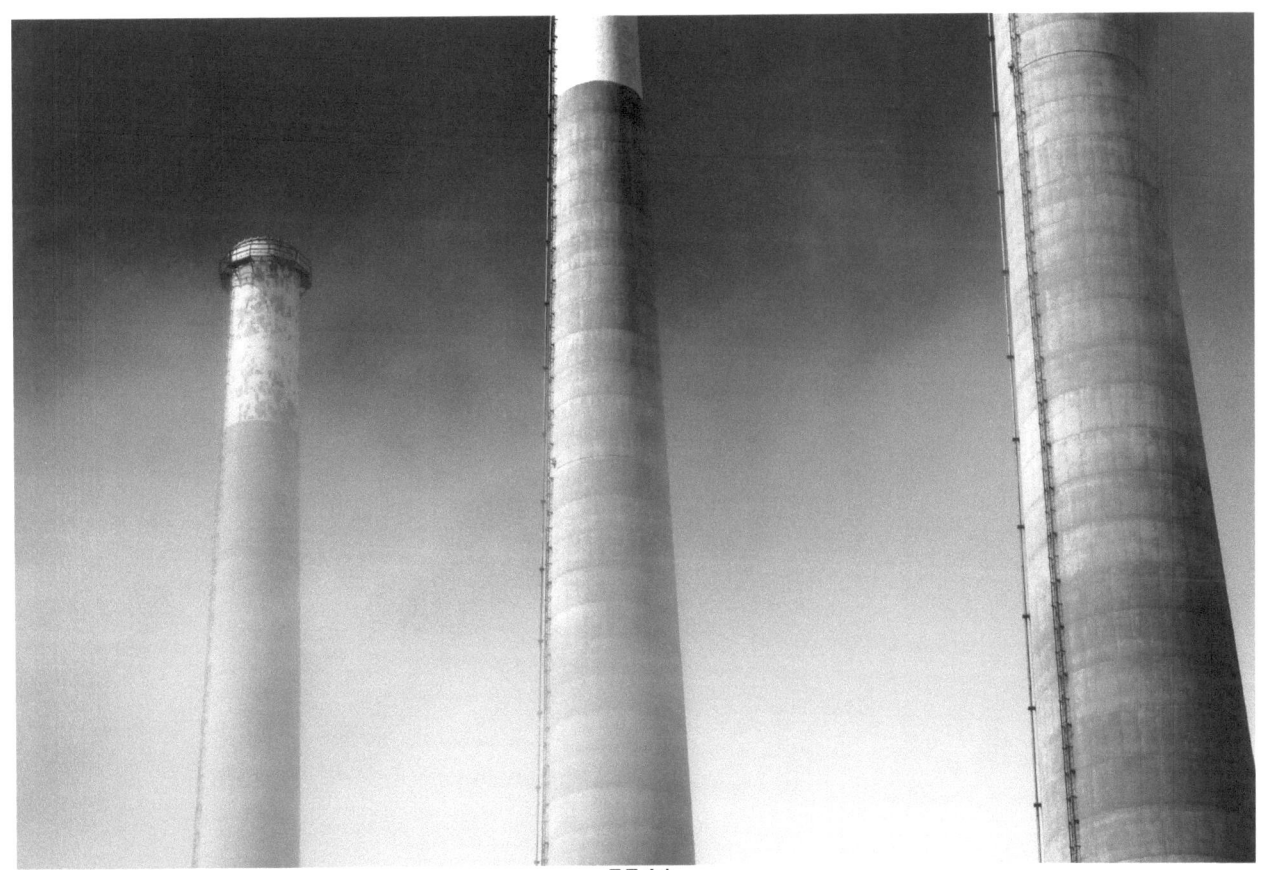

5541

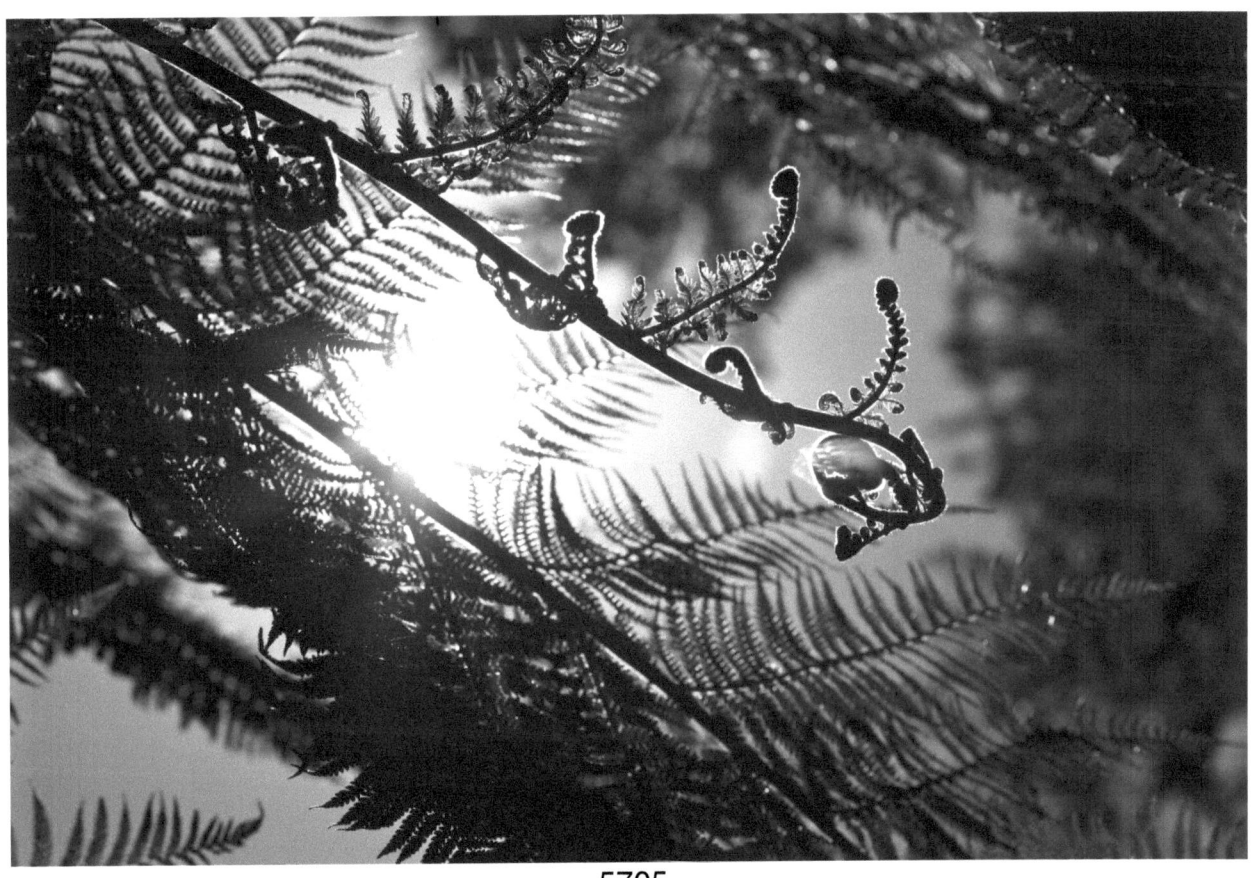

5705

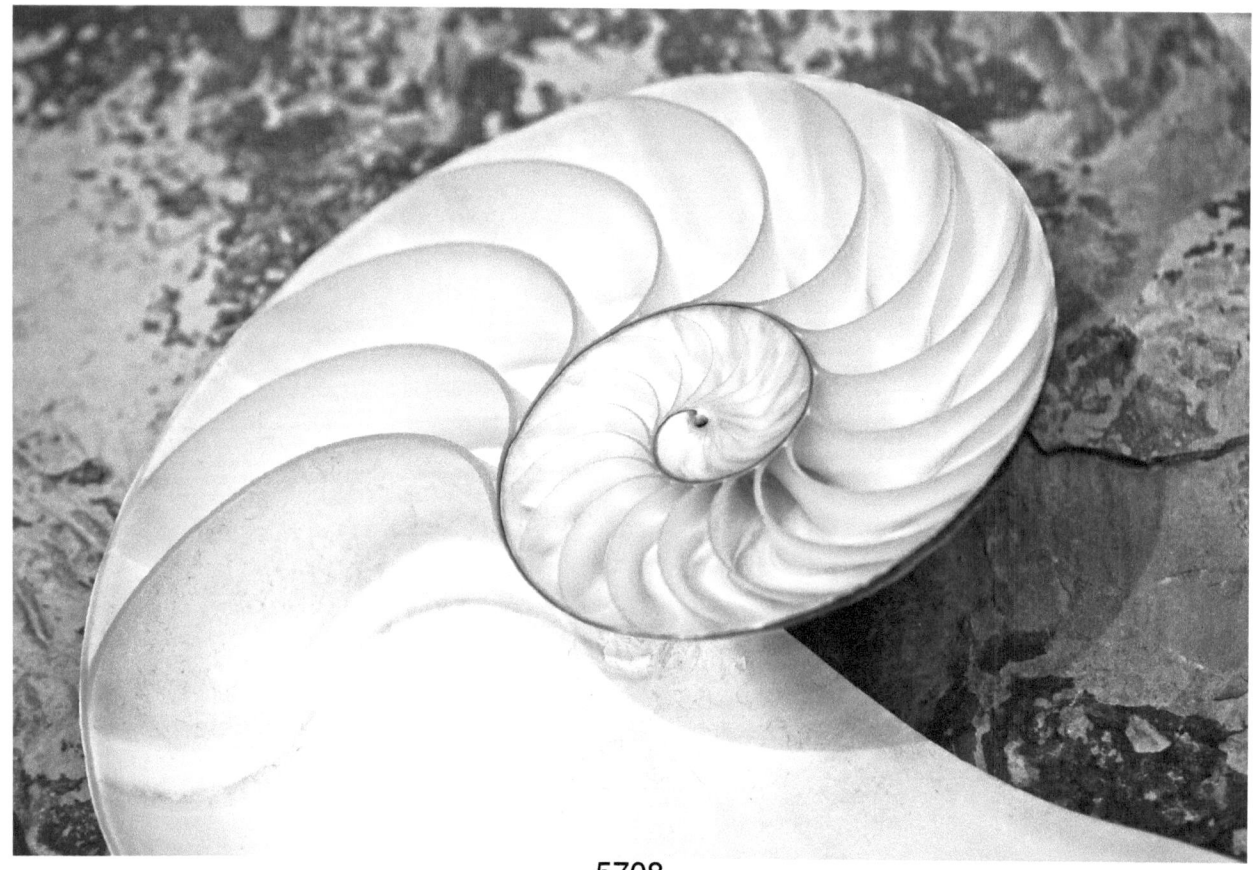

5708

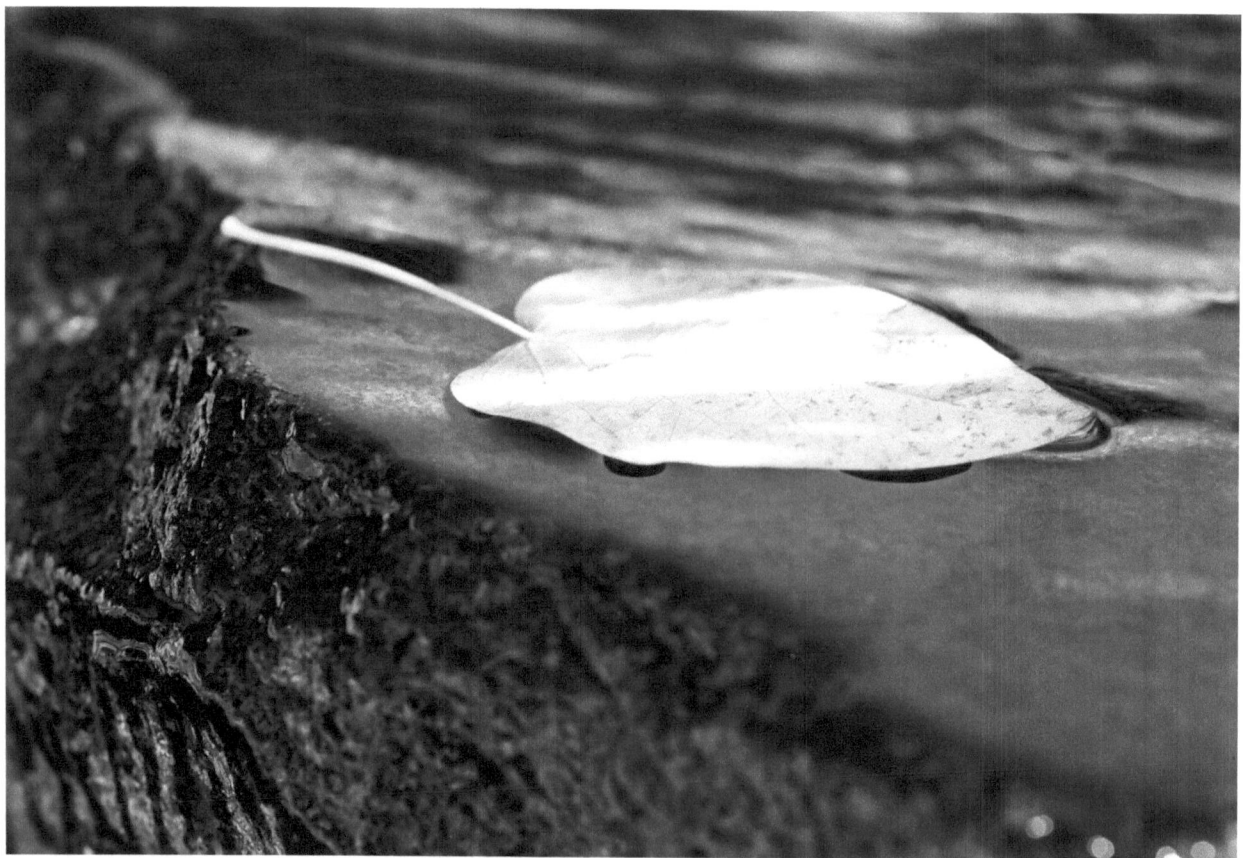

5750

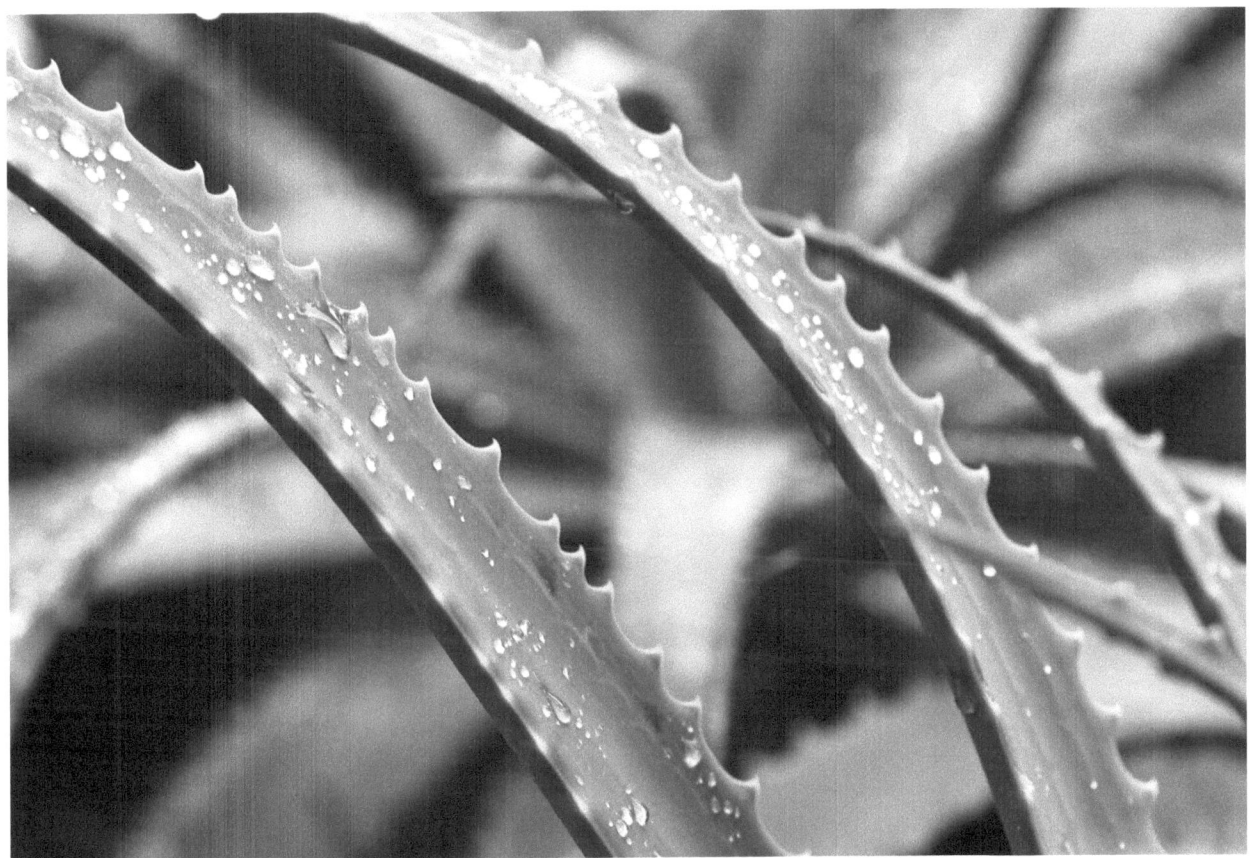

5784

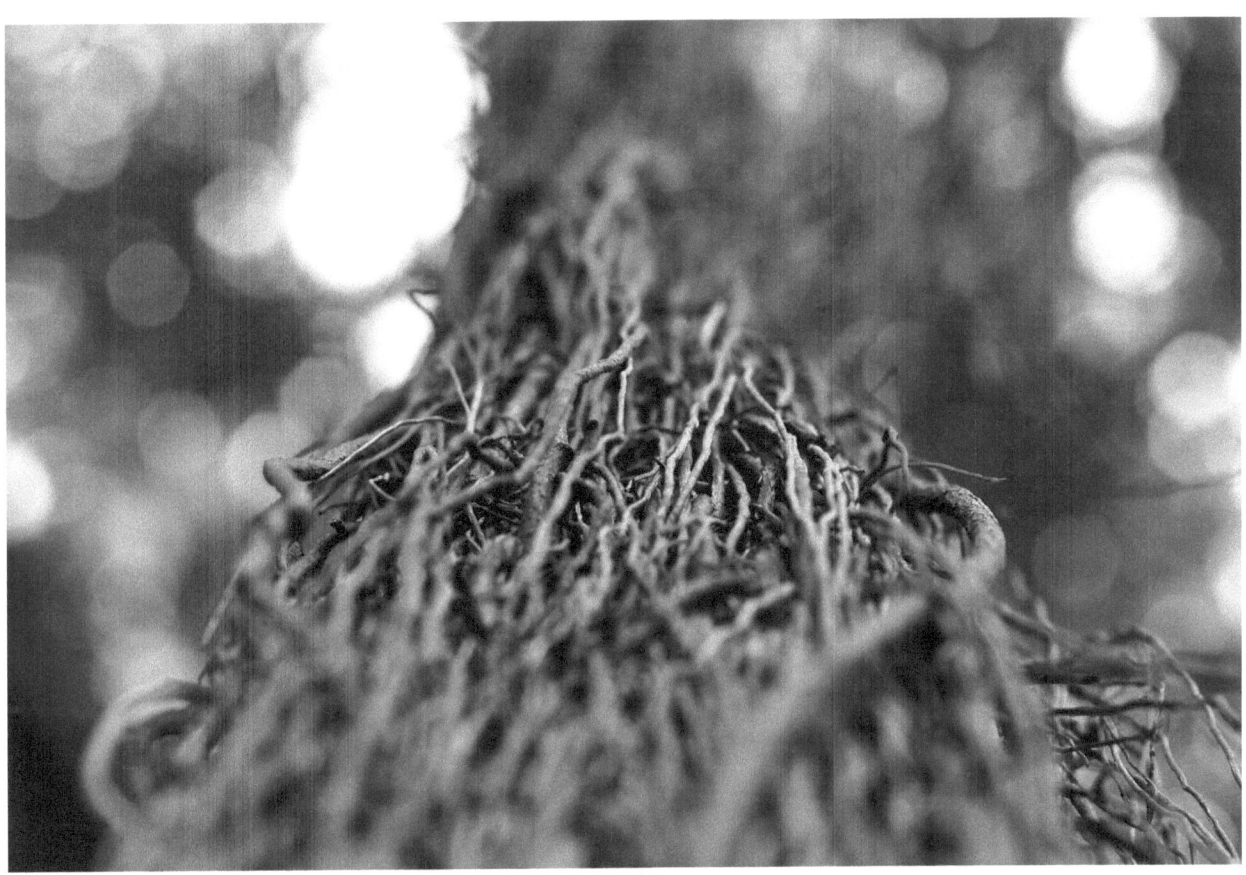

5811

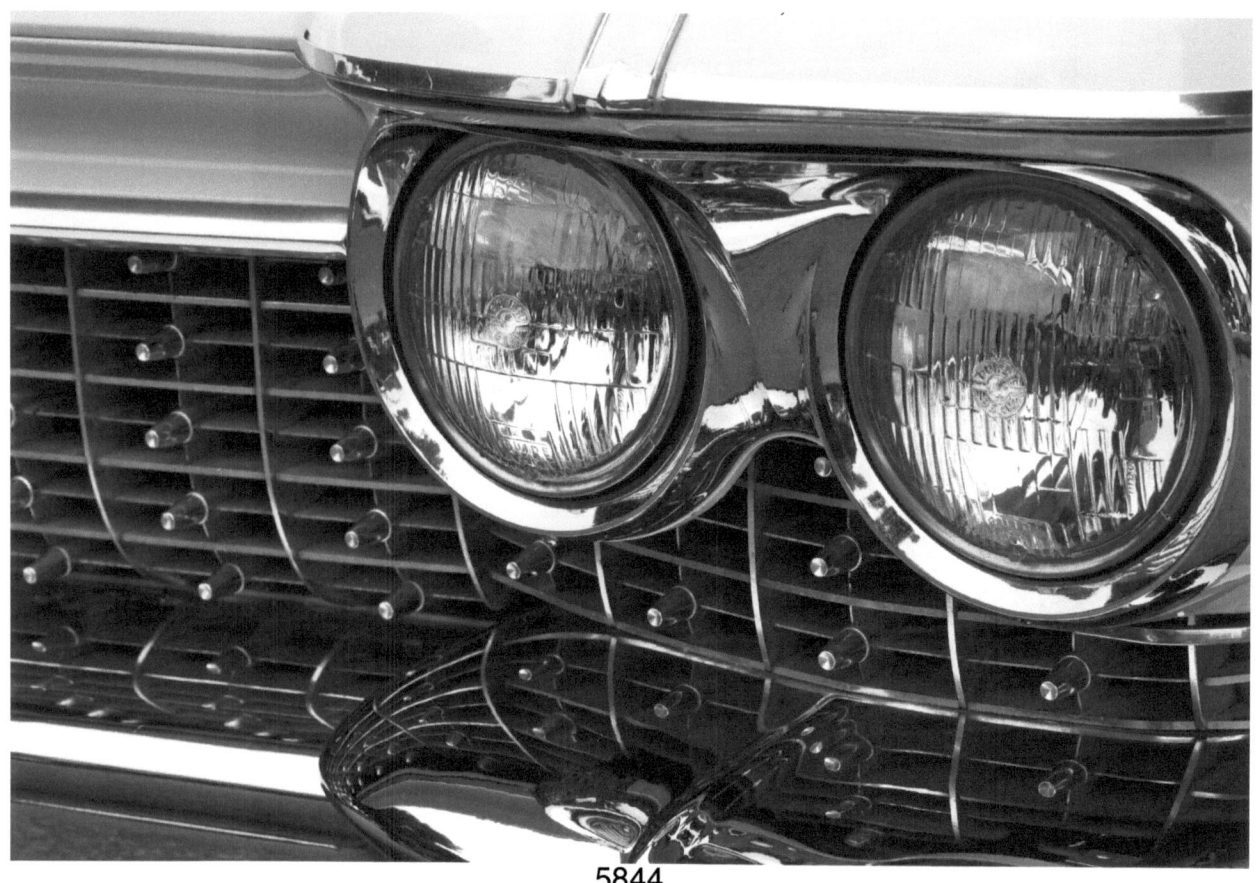

5844

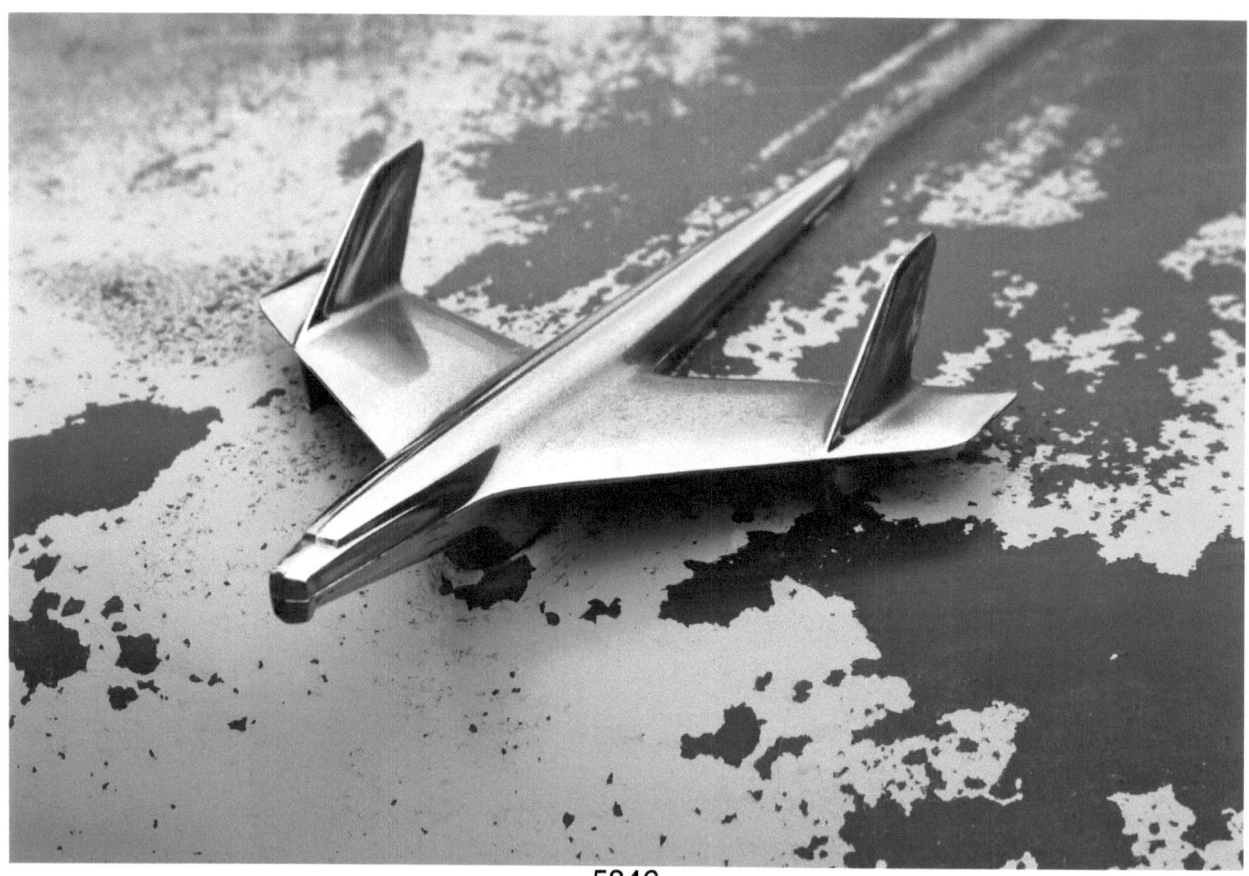

5846

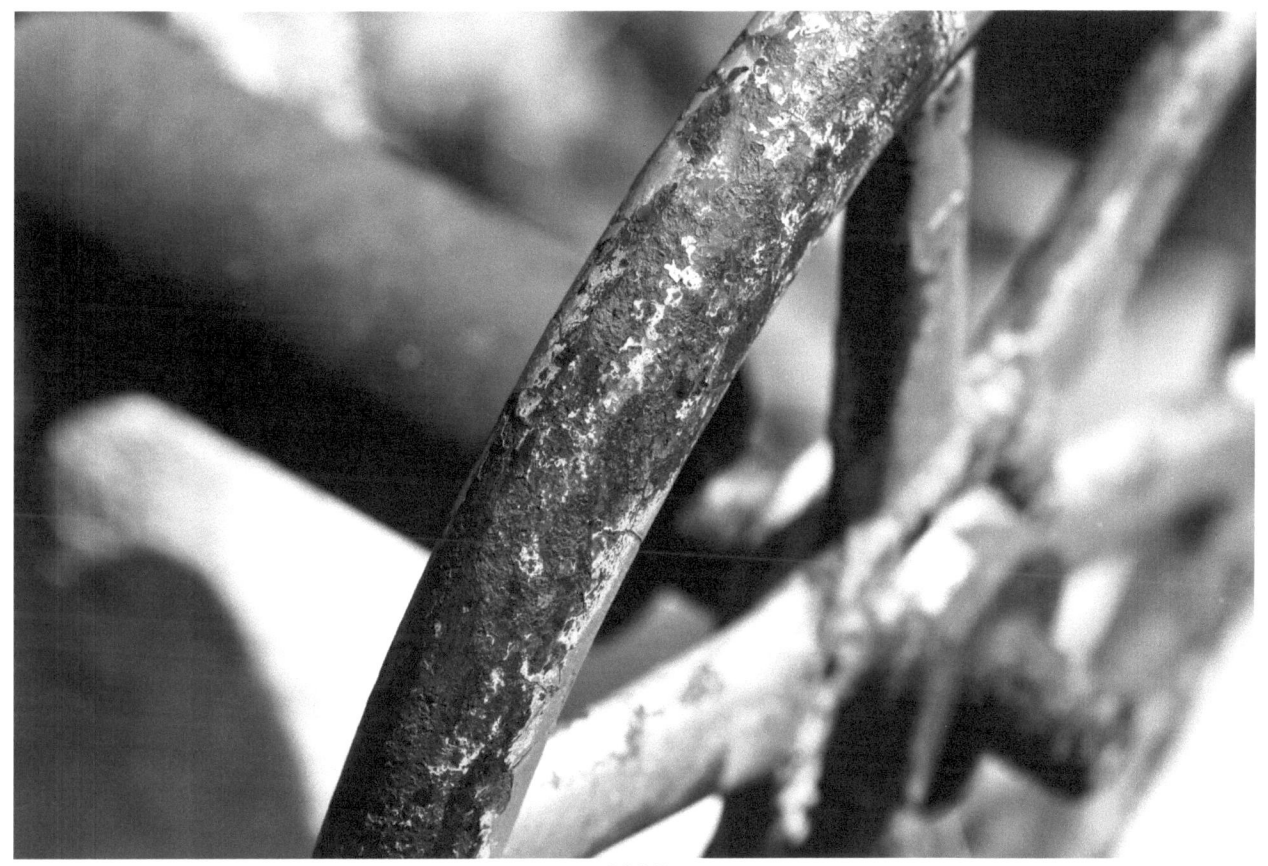

6095

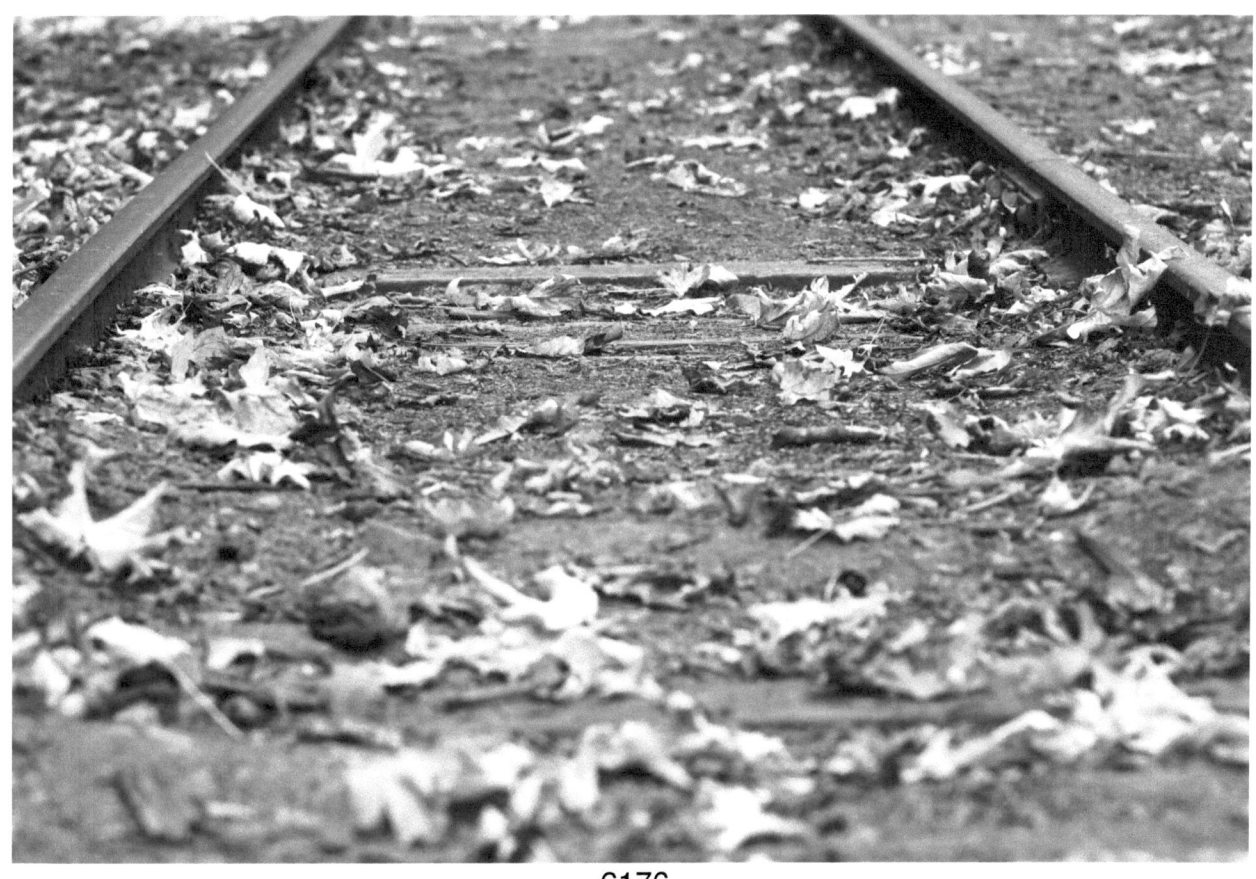

6176

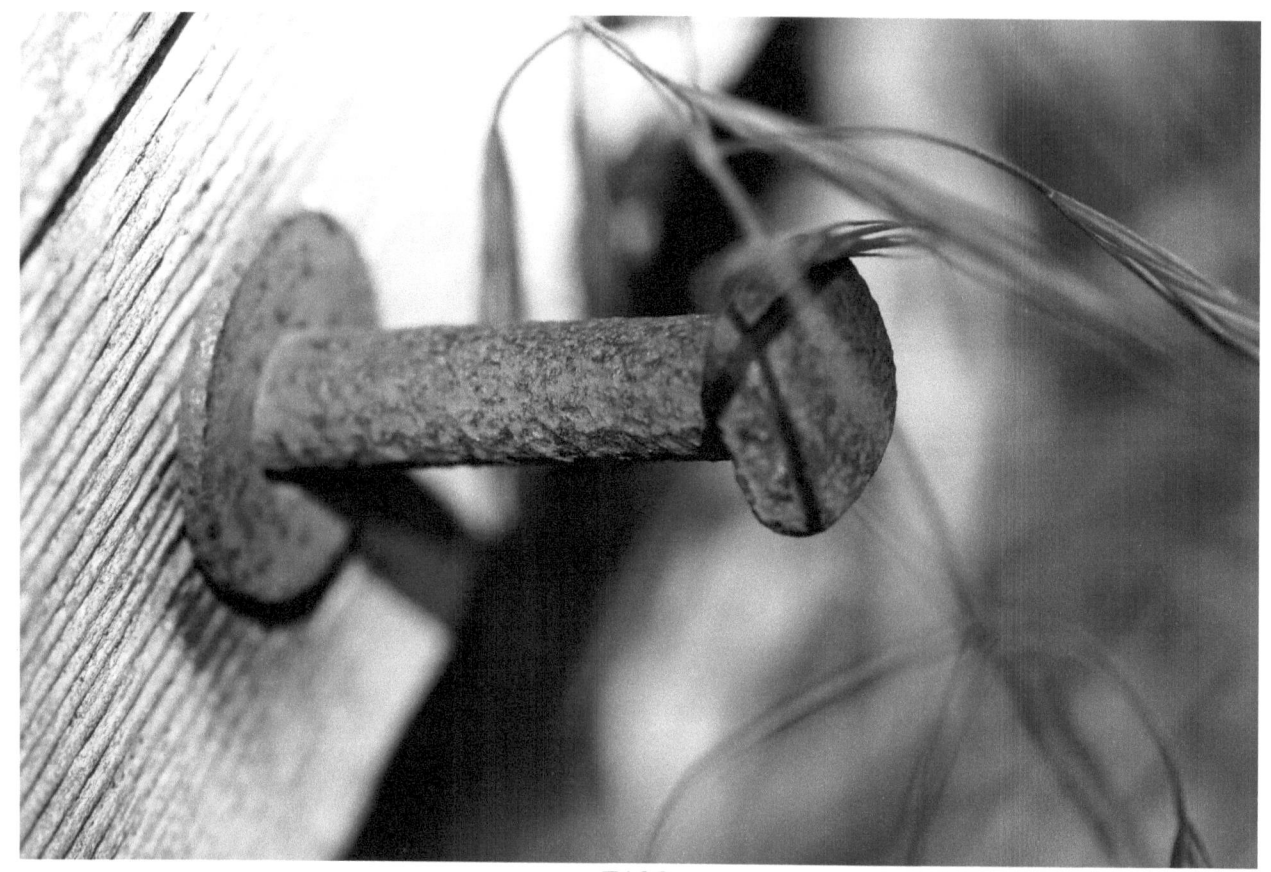

7182

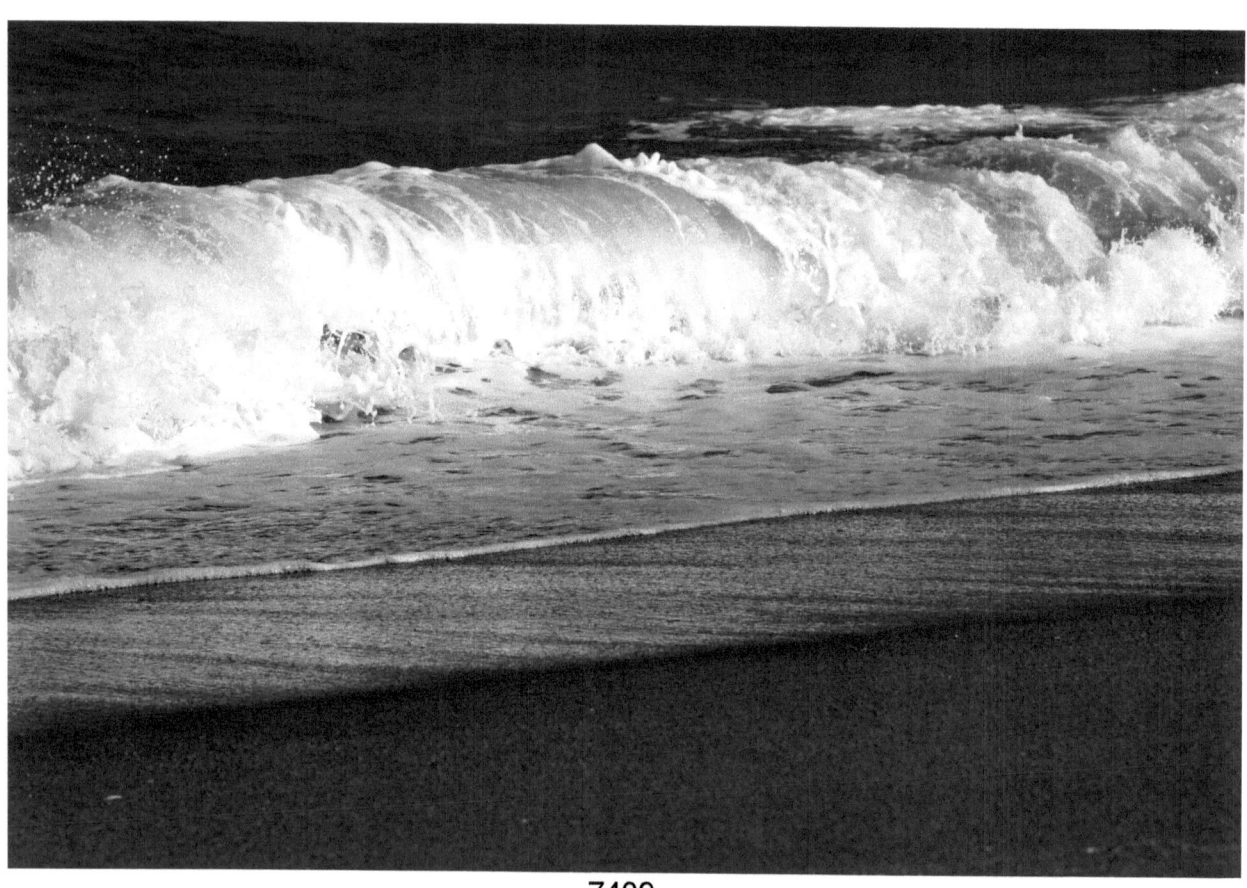

7409

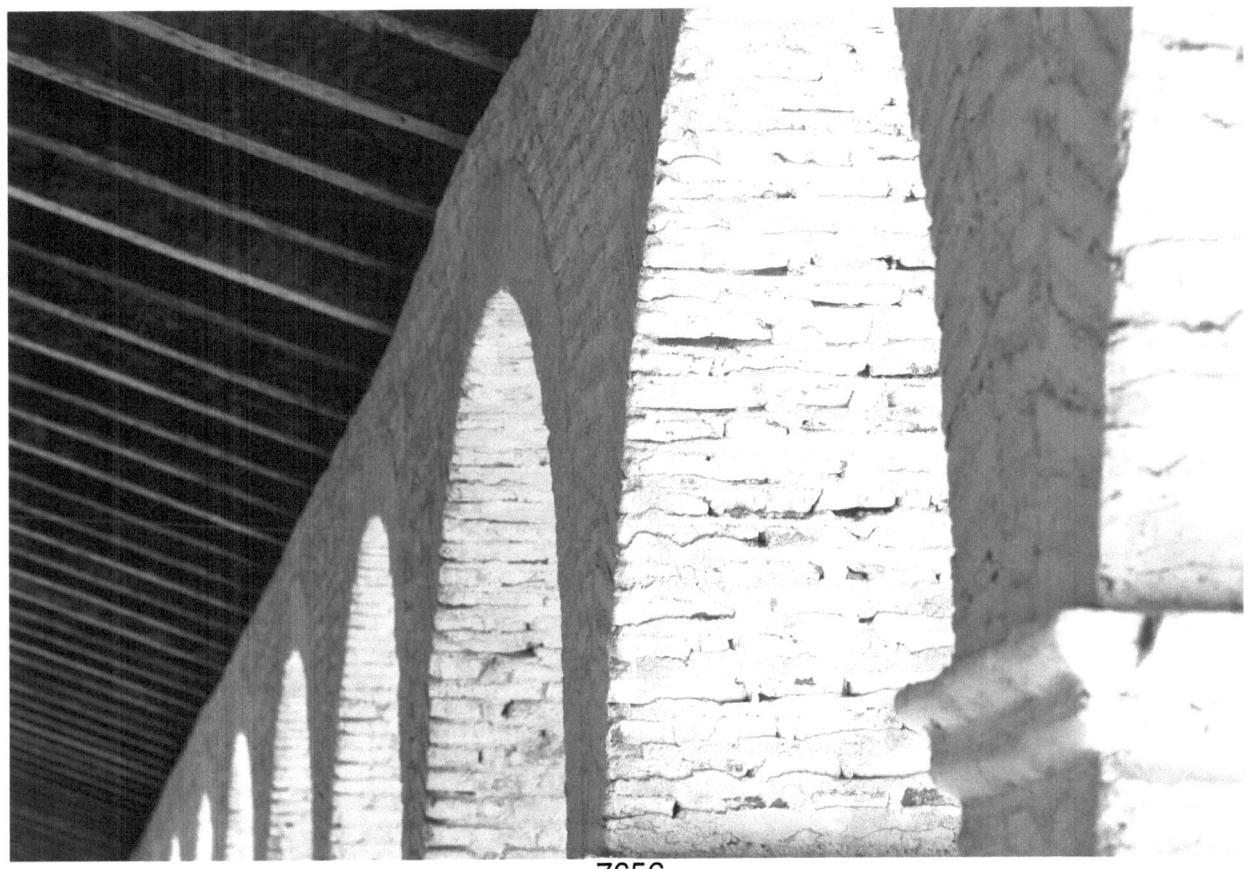

7656

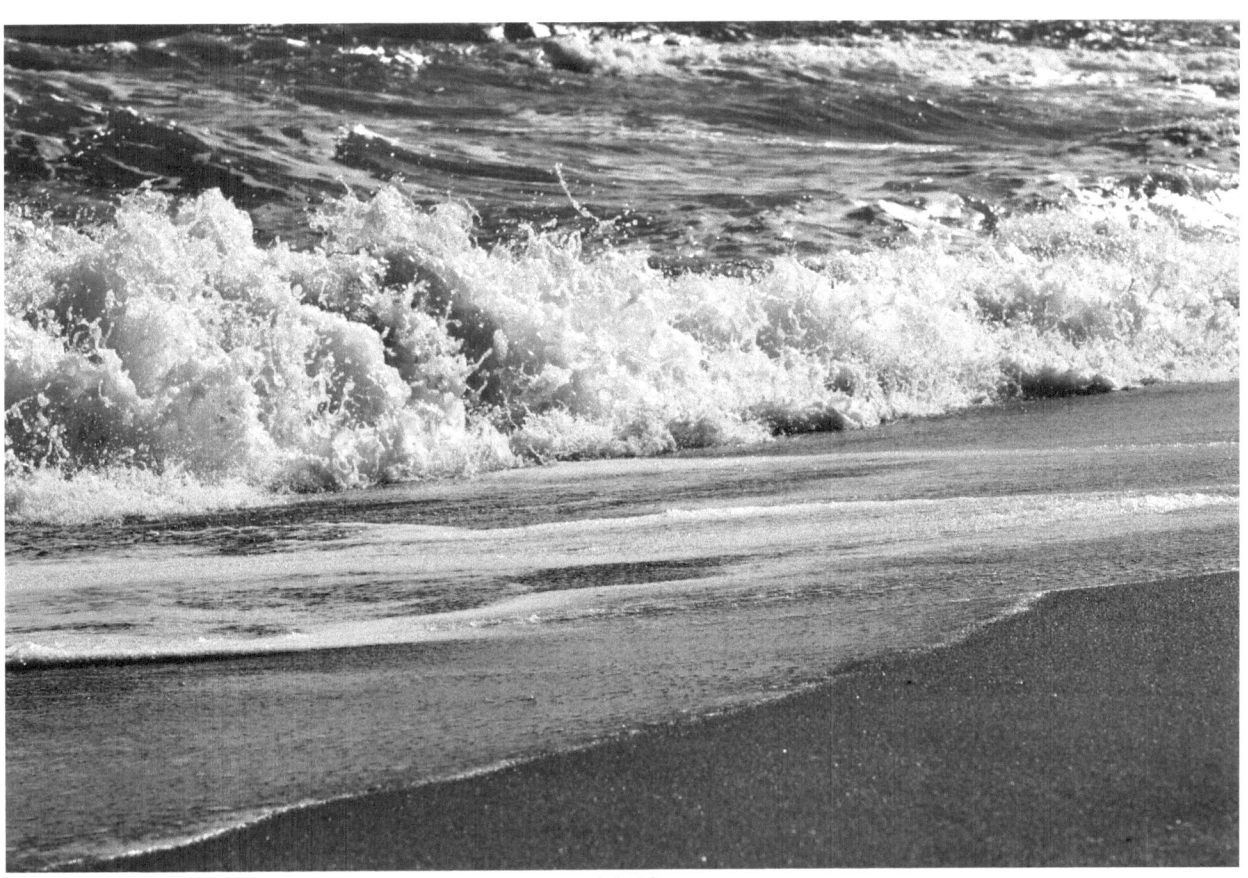

8079

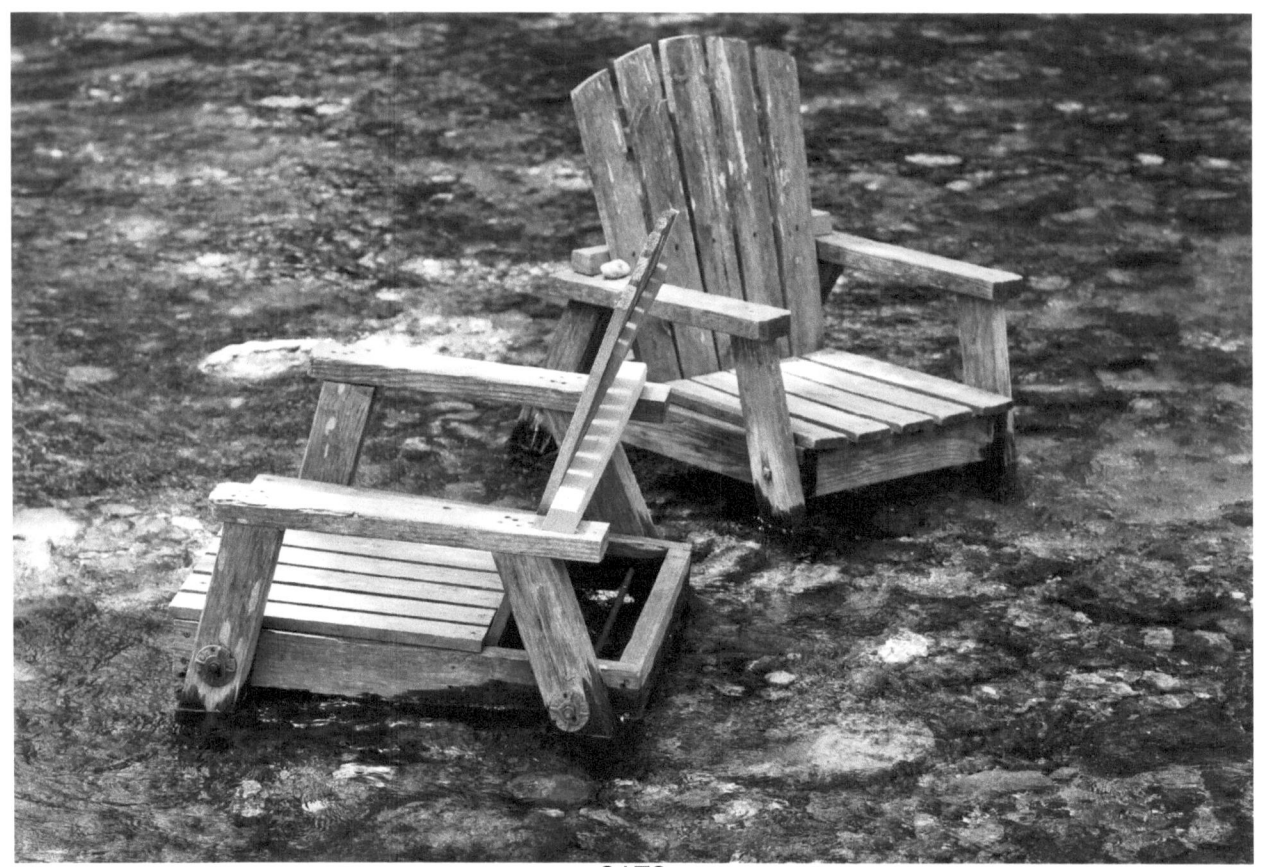

8173

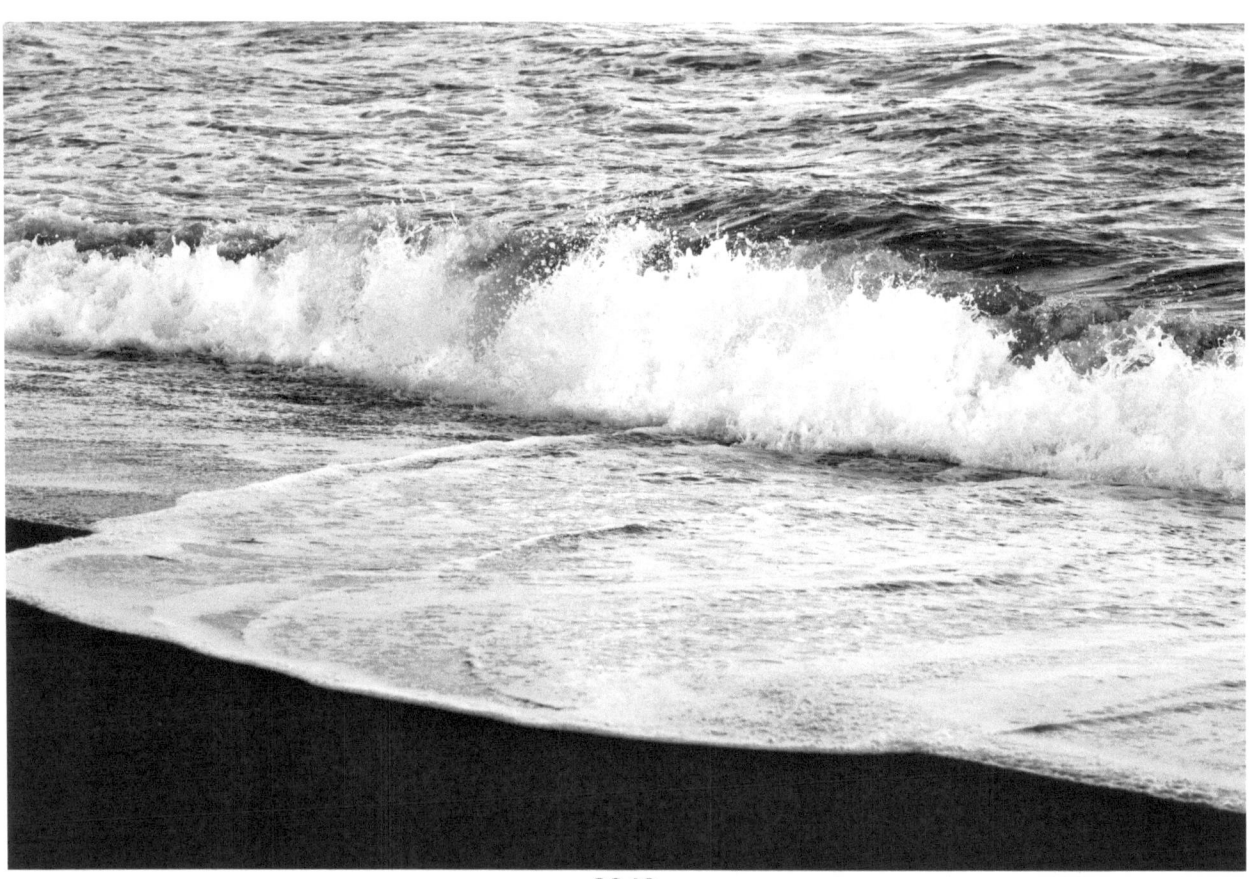

8249

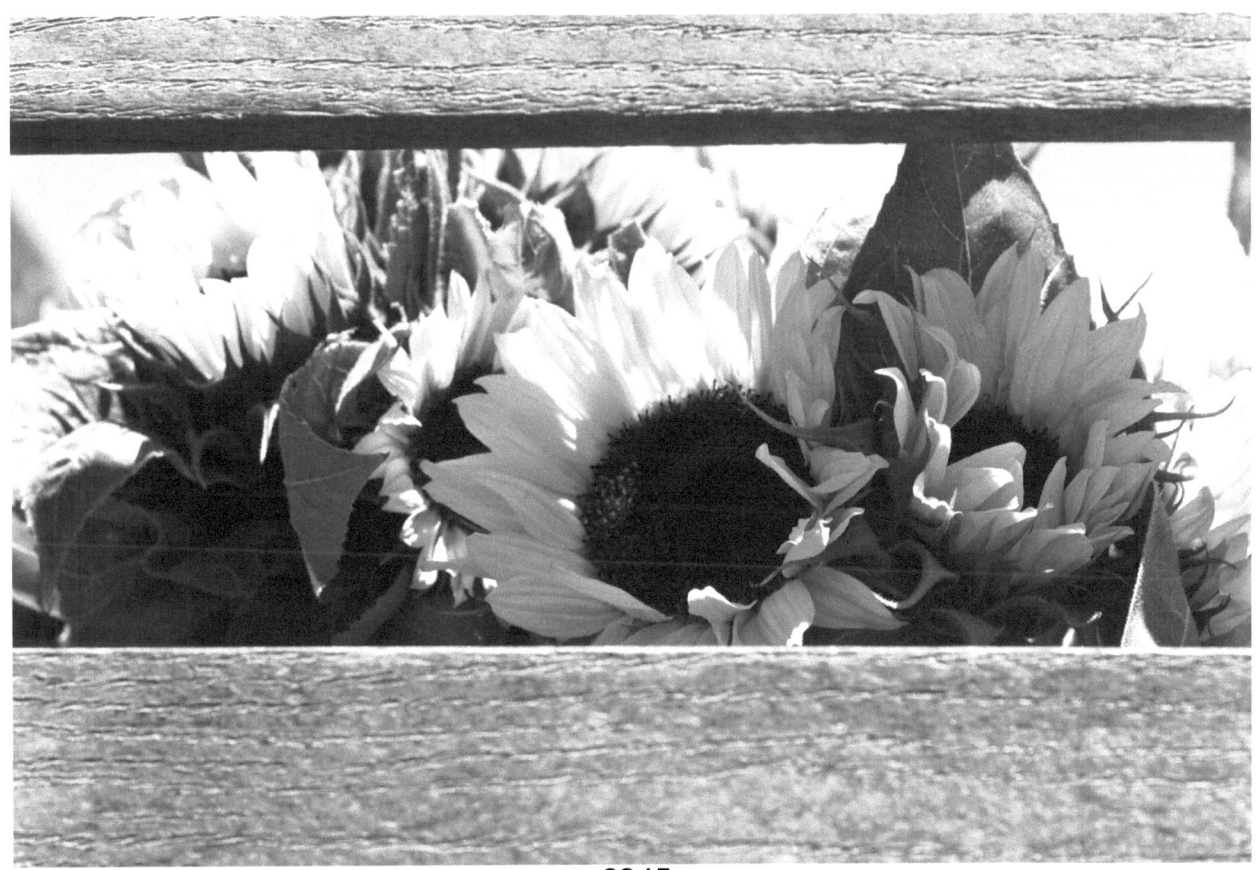

8345

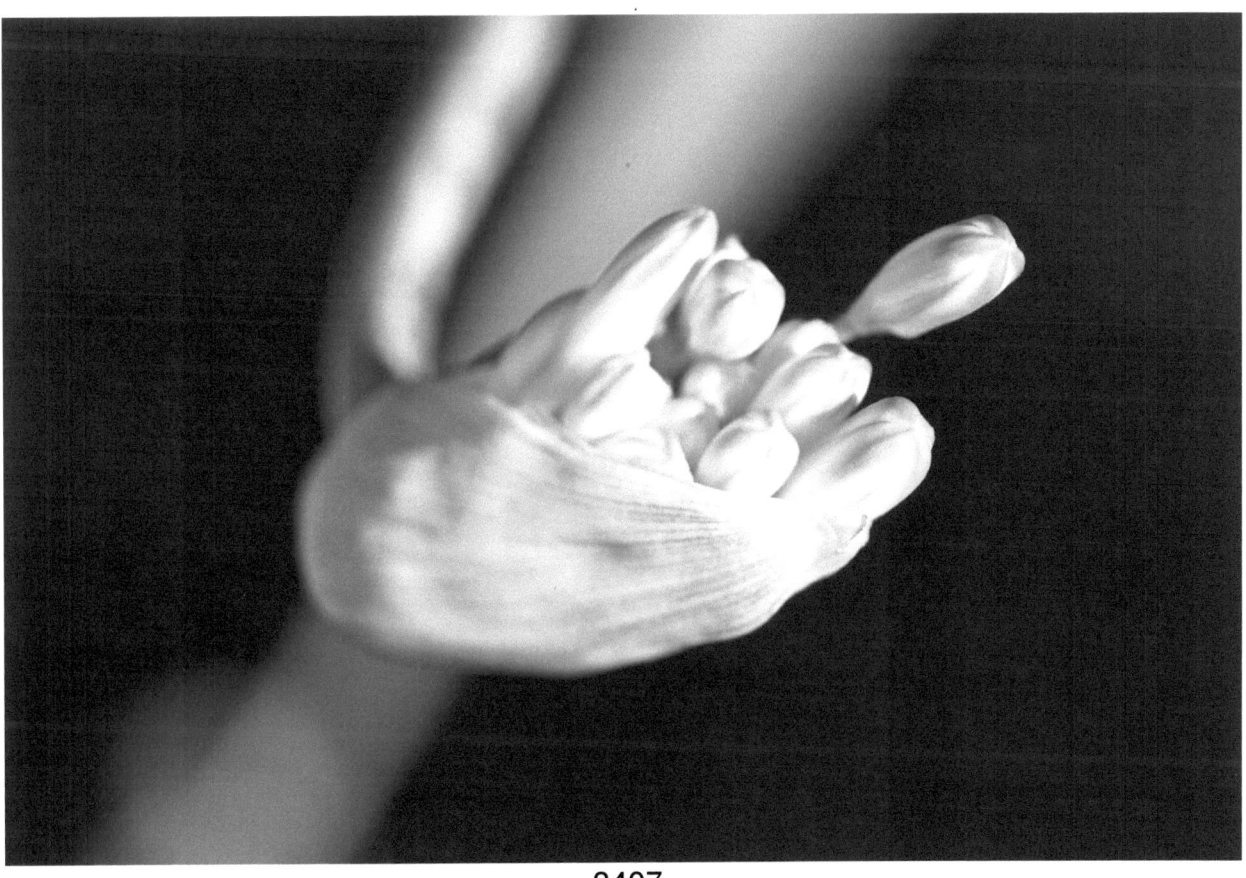

8407

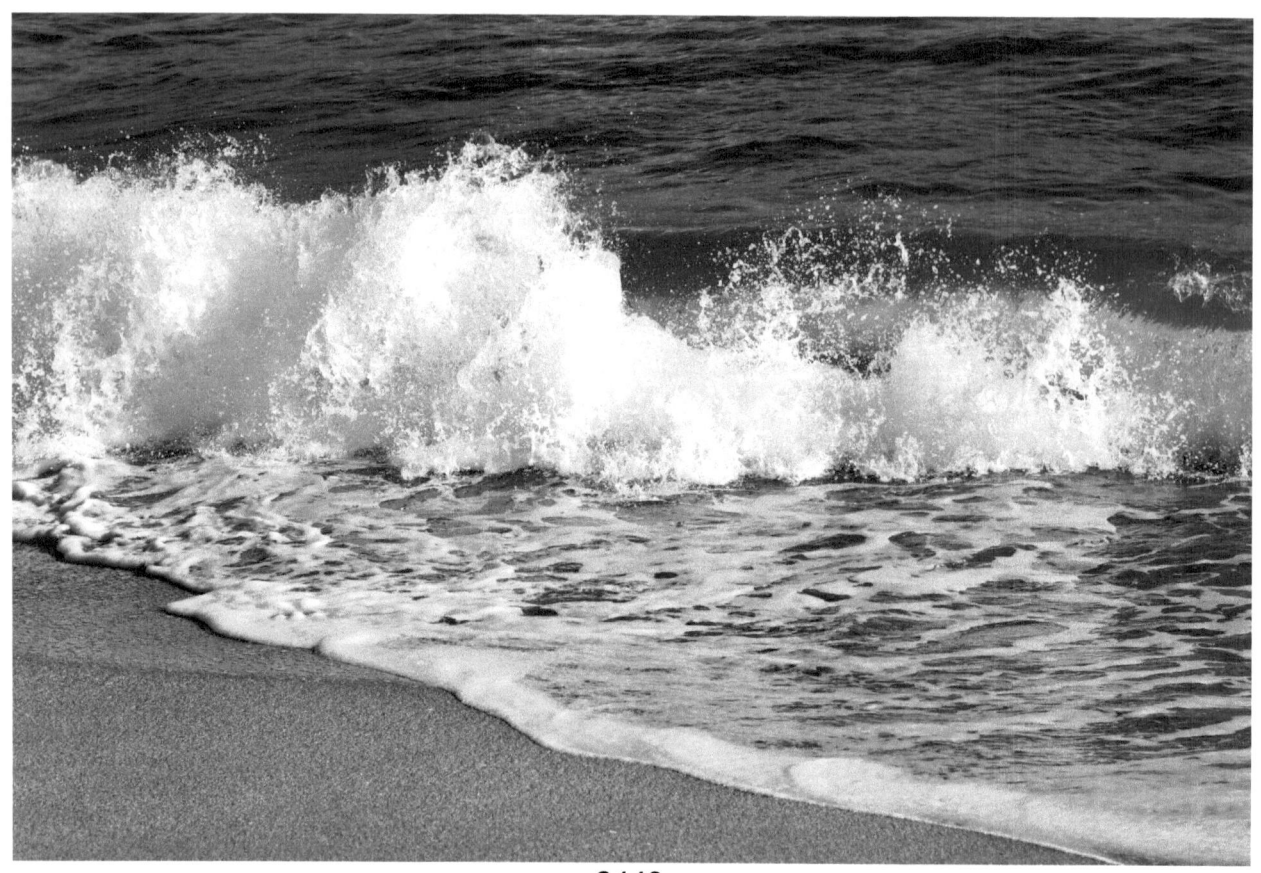

8449

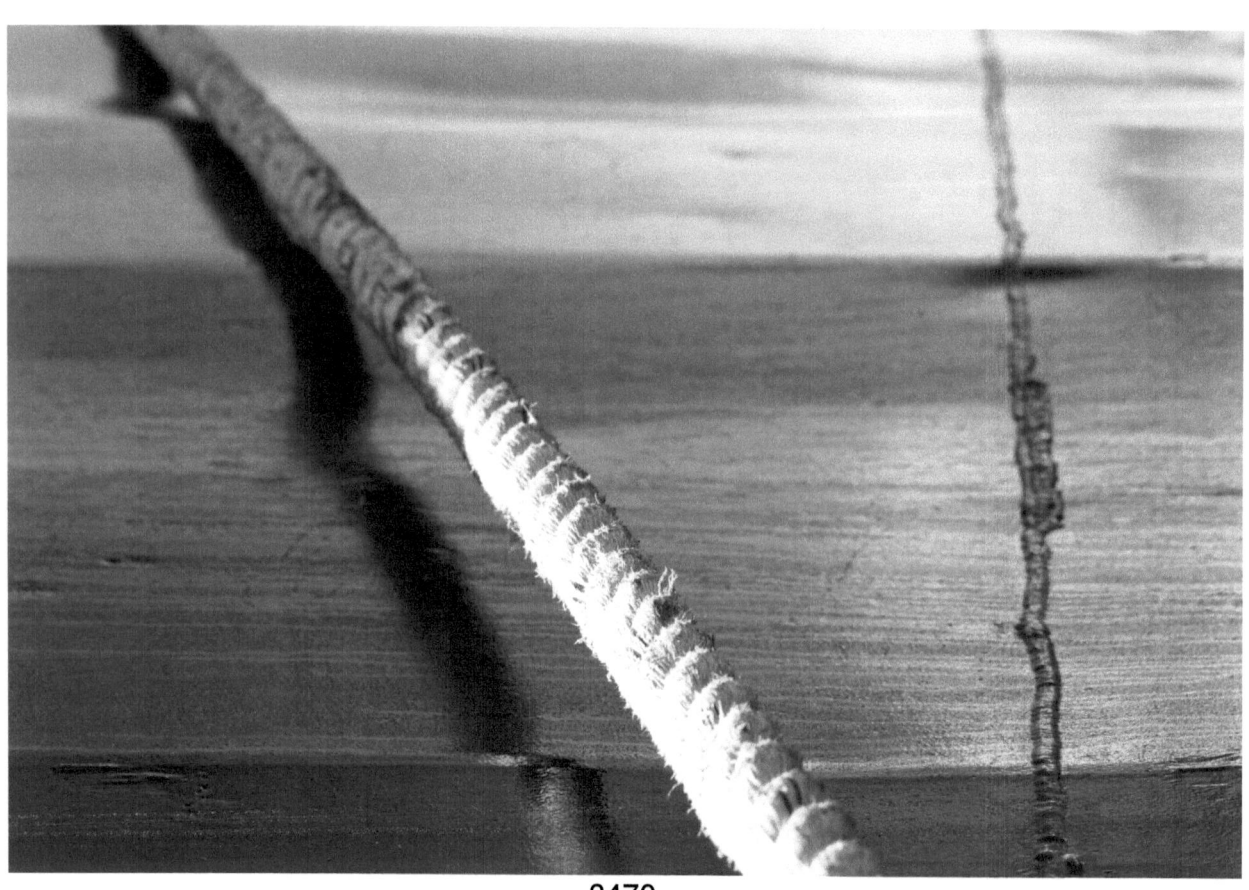

8470

8471

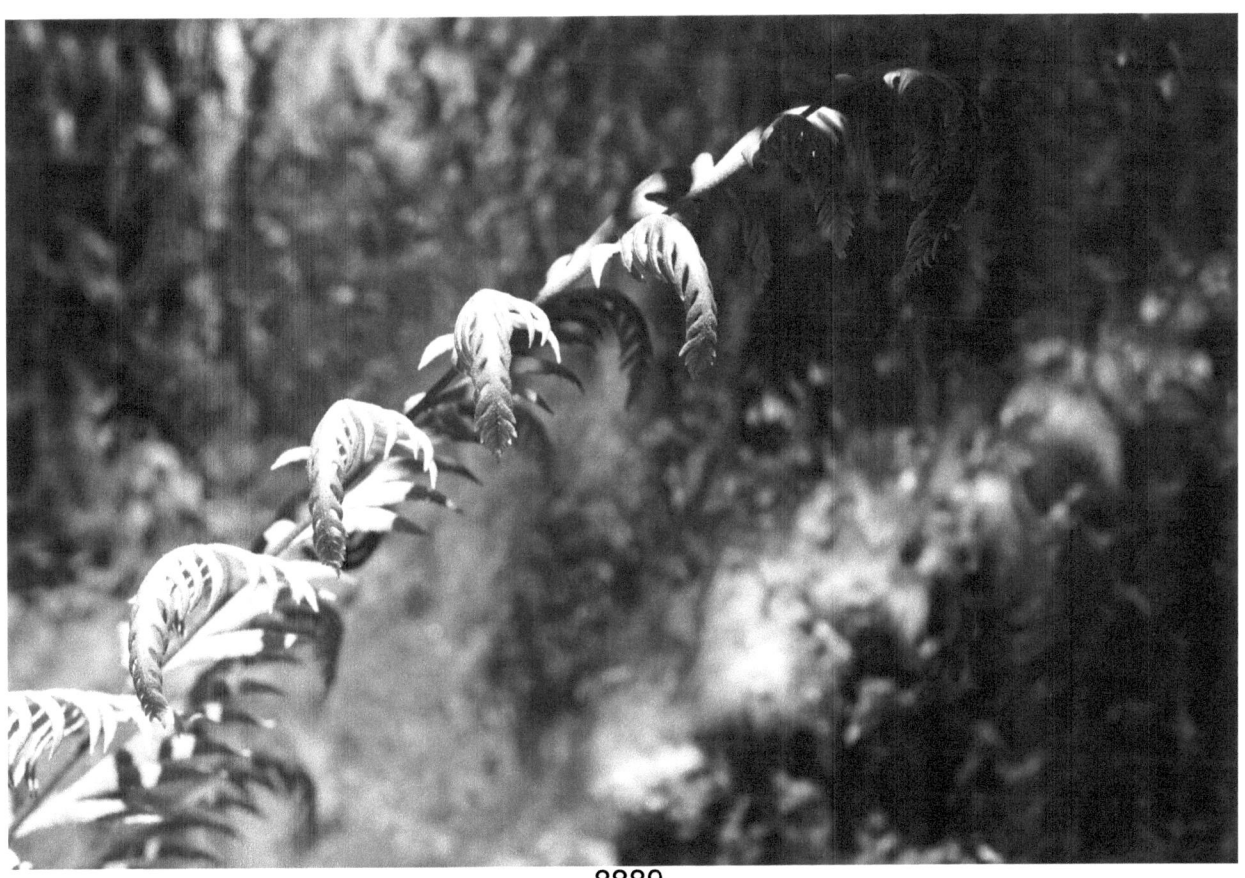

8889

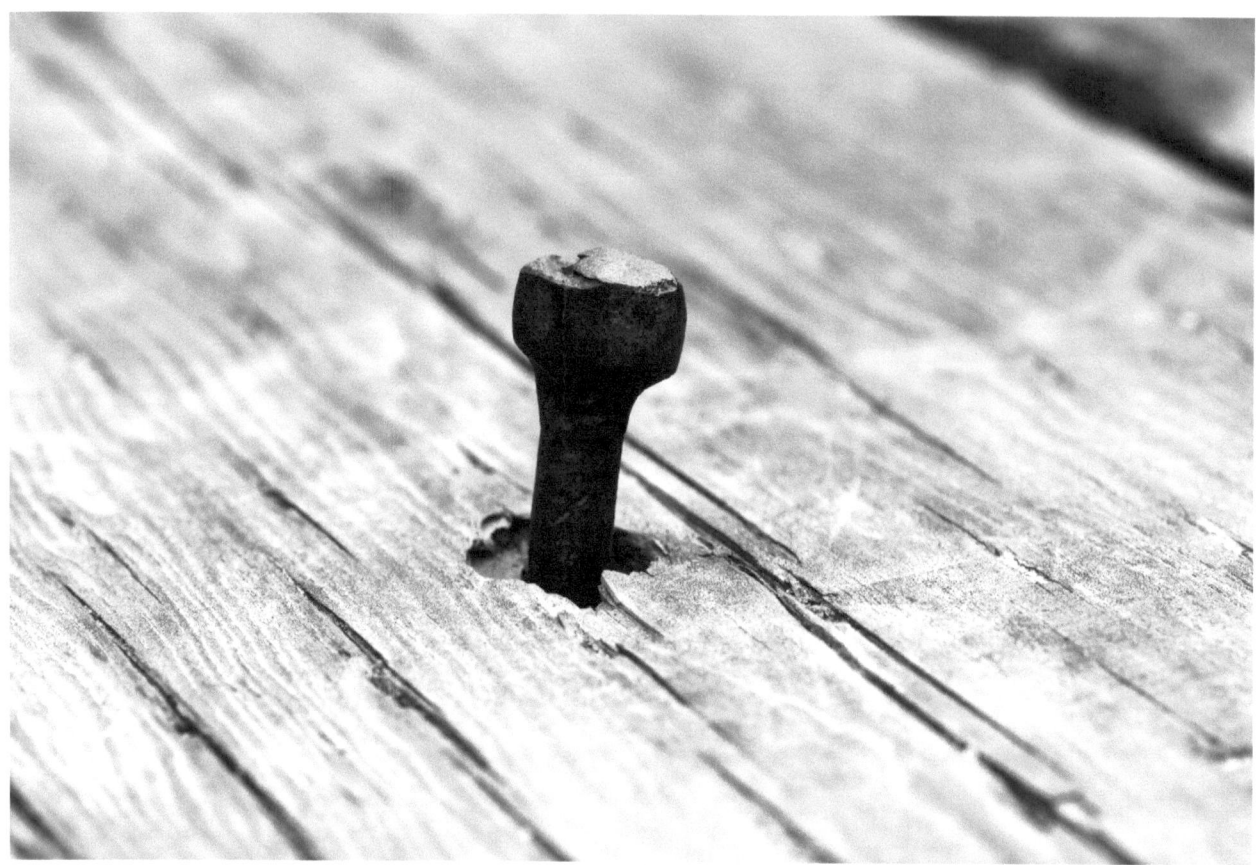

9024

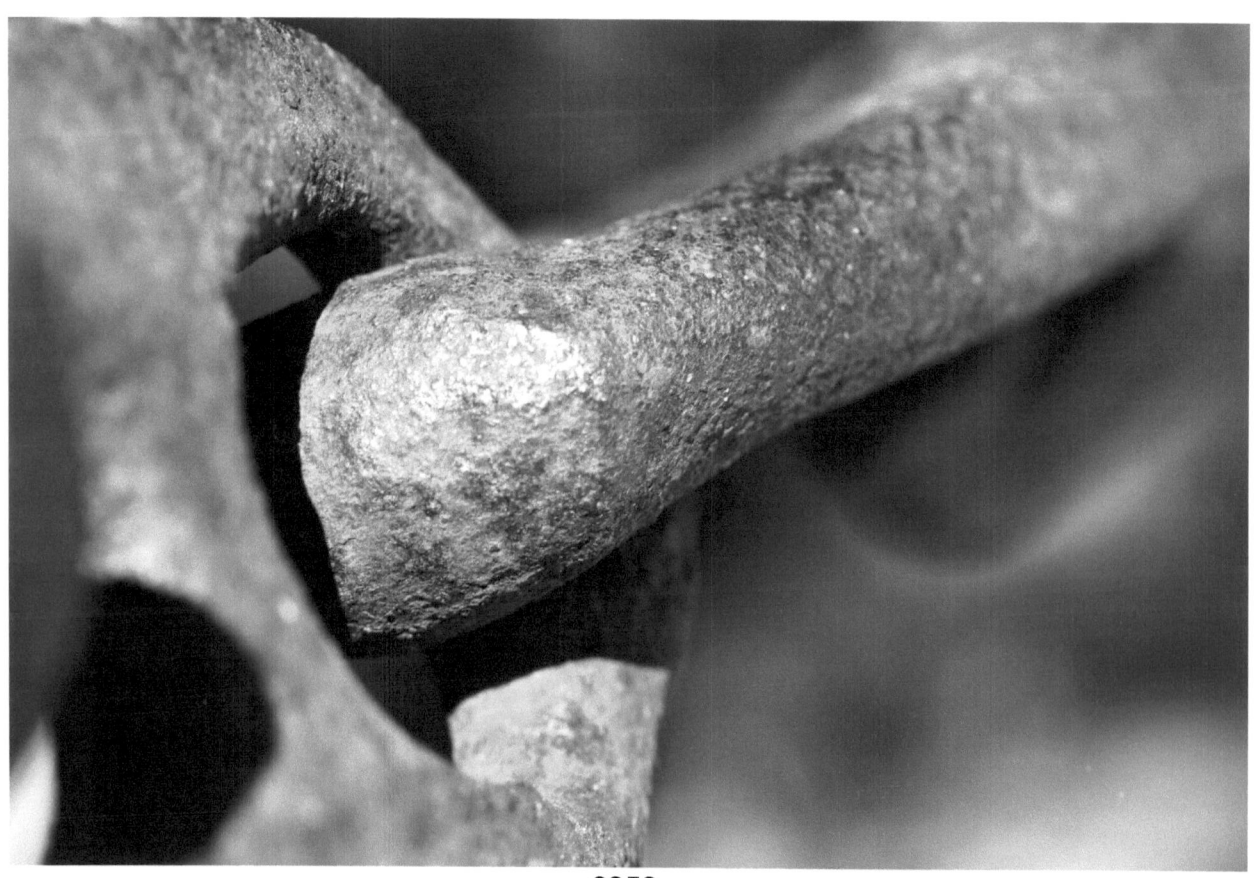

9353

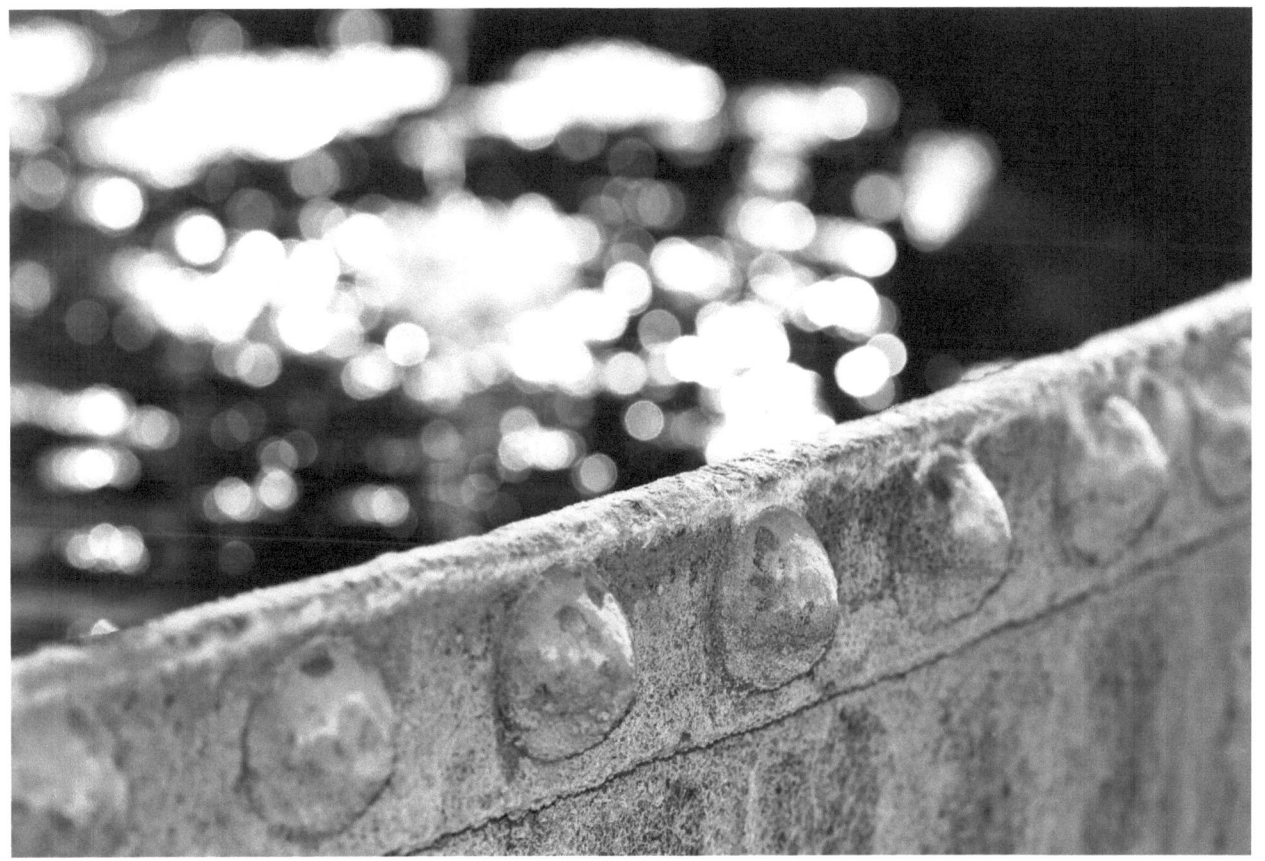

9430

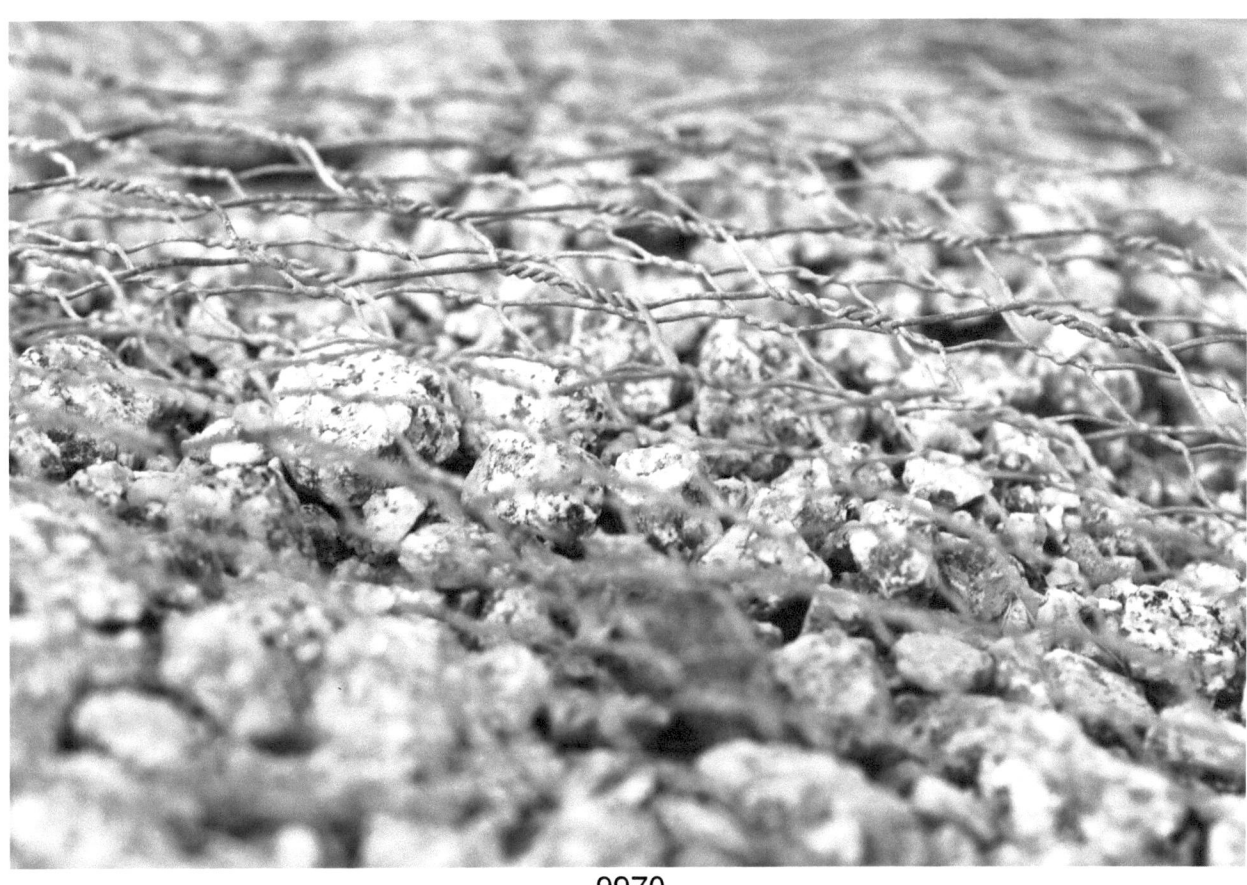

9970

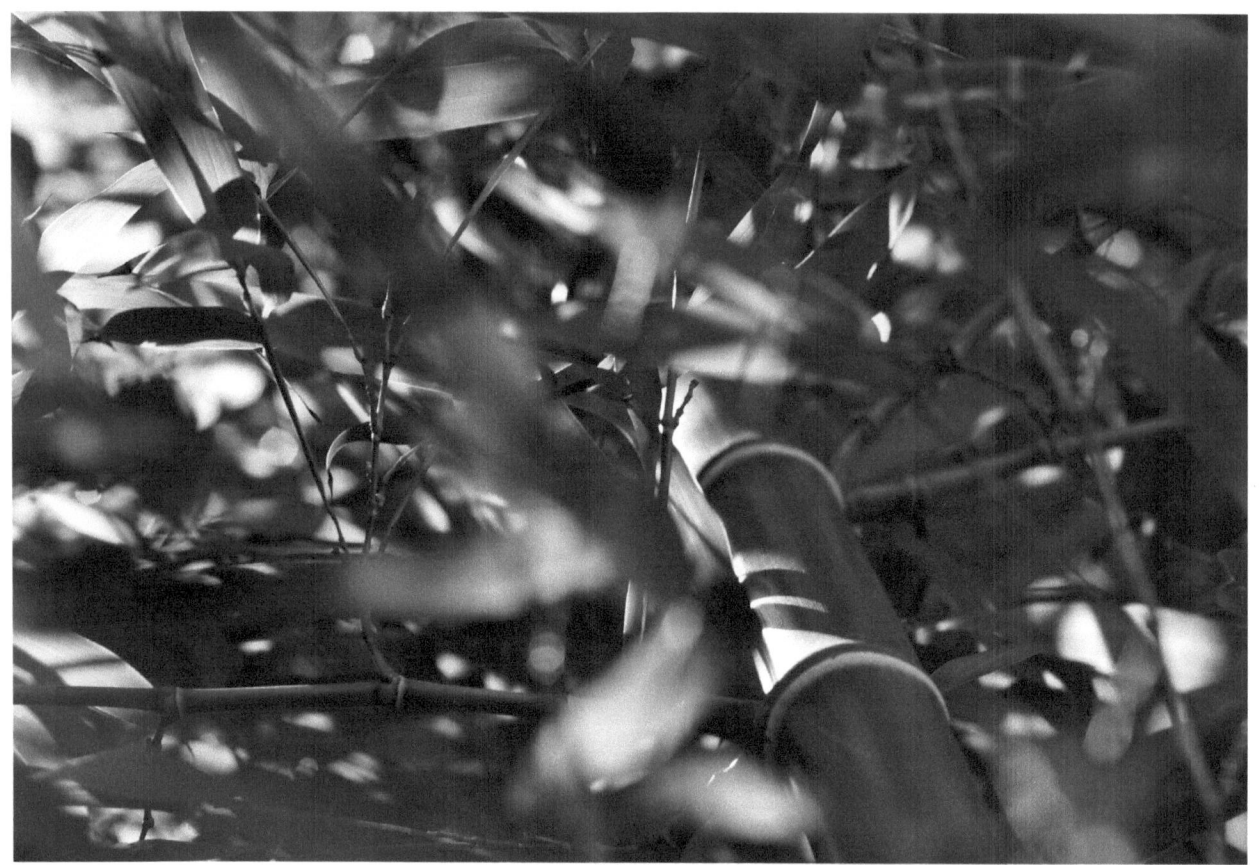

9975

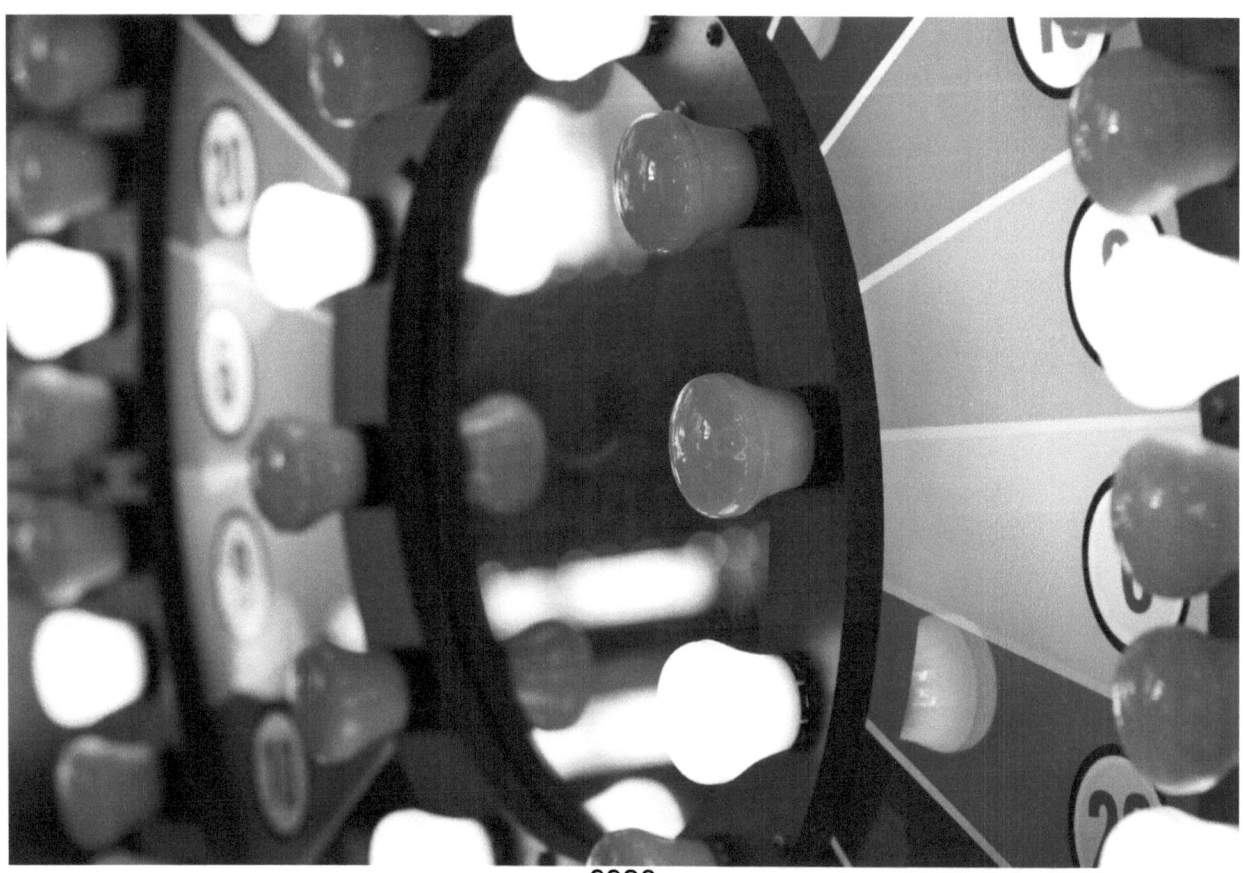

9980

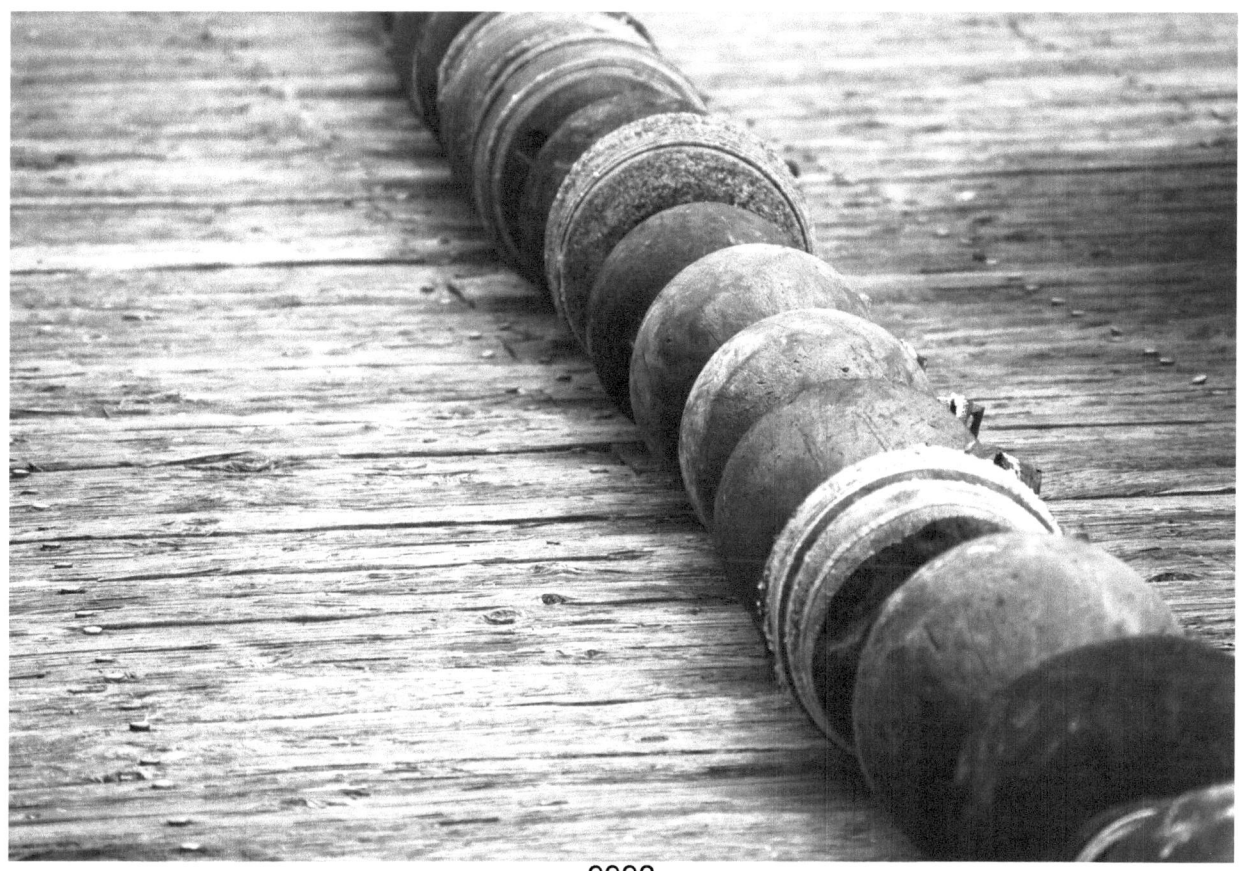

9998

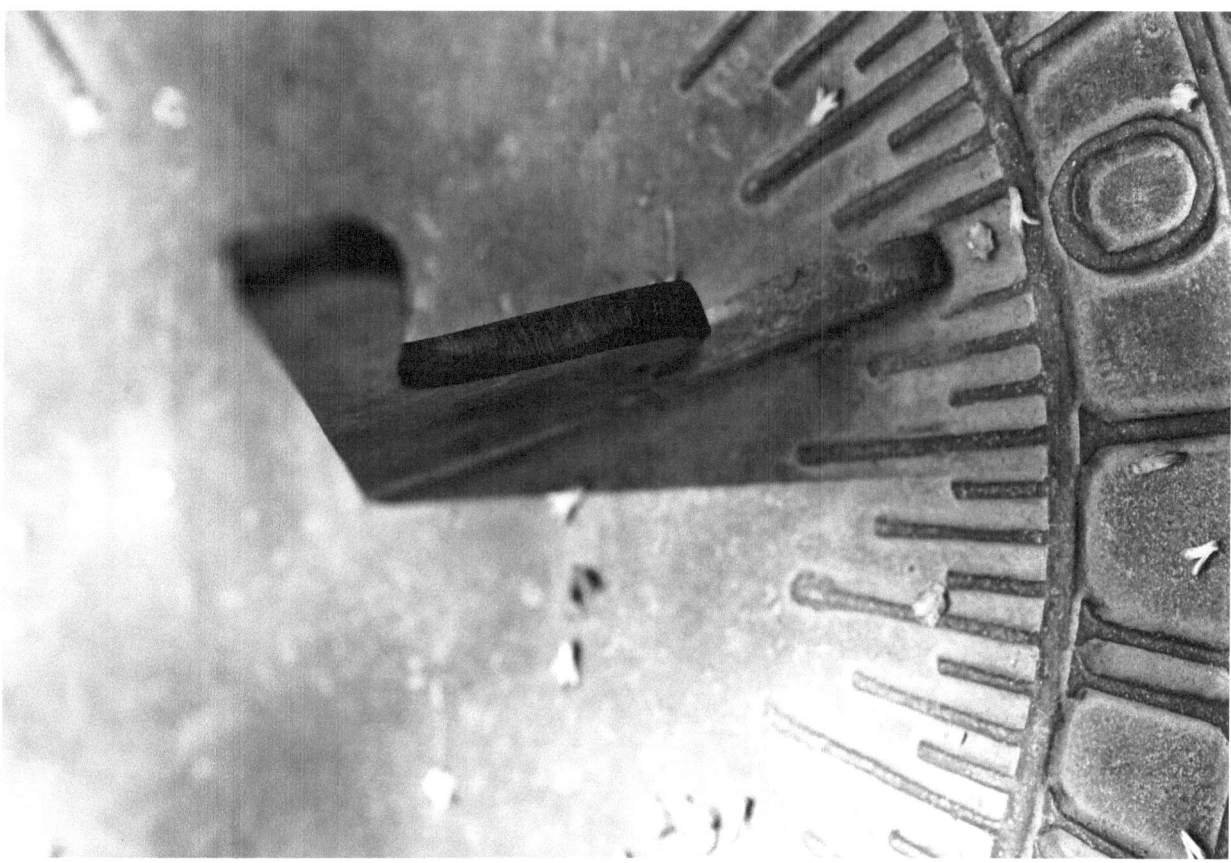

10002